Management, Organisations and Artificial Intelligence

This book combines academic research with practical guidelines in methods and techniques to supplement existing knowledge relating to organizational management in the era of digital acceleration. It offers a simple layout with concise but rich content presented in an engaging, accessible style and the authors' holistic approach is unique in the field.

From a universalist perspective, the book examines and analyzes the development of, among others, Industry 4.0, artificial intelligence (AI), AI 2.0, AI systems and platforms, algorithmics, new paradigms of organization management, business ecosystems, data processing models in AI-based organizations and AI strategies in the global perspective. An additional strength of the book is its relevance and contemporary nature, featuring information, data, forecasts or scenarios reaching up to 2030. How does one build, step by step, an organization that will be based on artificial intelligence technology and gain measurable benefits from it, for instance, as a result of its involvement in the creation of the so-called mesh ecosystem? The answer to this and many other pertinent questions are provided in this book.

This timely and important book will appeal to scholars and students across the fields of organizational management and innovation and technology management, as well as managers, educators, scientists, entrepreneurs, innovators and more.

Piotr Buła is Associate Professor and Head of the International Management Department at Cracow University of Economics (CUE), Poland, Vice-Rector for Projects and Cooperation (CUE), former Director of Cracow School of Business (CUE), Senior Research Professor in Business Management Department at the University of Johannesburg, South Africa, and Grand Valley State University scholarship holder. He is the author or co-author of more than 170 publications in economics and management. His research interests focus on aspects related to the application of artificial intelligence and neuromanagement, risk management, internal audit, international management and logistics. A member of international organizations associating professors and business practitioners in the management area: EFMD, CEEMAN, IMDA, GBATA, EIBA, GSSI, IAMB, EECSA, SAIMS.

Bartosz Niedzielski is Assistant Professor at Cracow University of Economics, Poland. He studied and conducted scientific activities, among other subjects, at the University of Greenwich, University of Oxford, UK, London School of Economics, UK, Deggendorf Institute of Technology, Germany, and Jagiellonian University, Poland. He has over 10 years of professional experience gained in global corporations in the BPO/SCC sector (mainly at HSBC). His research interests focus on aspects related to the application of artificial intelligence in organizations, management and internal audit. He is the author or co-author of more than 50 scientific publications in economics and management.

RIOT!

Routledge Studies in Innovation, Organizations and Technology

Management in the Age of Digital Business Complexity
Edited by Bill McKelvey with Renata Kaminska, Maria Paz Salmador and Nadine Escoffier

Citizen Activities in Energy Transition
User Innovation, New Communities, and the Shaping of a Sustainable Future
Sampsa Hyysalo

How Ideas Move
Theories and Models of Translation in Organizations
John Damm Scheuer

Managing IT for Innovation
Dynamic Capabilities and Competitive Advantage
Mitsuru Kodama

Technological Change and Industrial Transformation
Edited by Vicky Long and Magnus Holmén

Sustainability, Technology and Innovation 4.0
Edited by Zbigniew Makieła, Magdalena M. Stuss and Ryszard Borowiecki

Management and Information Technology after Digital Transformation
Edited by Peter Ekman, Peter Dahlin and Christina Keller

The Business Model Innovation Process
Preparation, Organization and Management
Yariv Taran, Harry Boer and Christian Nielsen

Management, Organisations and Artificial Intelligence
Where Theory Meets Practice
Piotr Buła and Bartosz Niedzielski

For more information about this series, please visit: www.routledge.com/Routledge-Studies-in-Innovation-Organizations-and-Technology/book-series/RIOT

Management, Organisations and Artificial Intelligence

Where Theory Meets Practice

Piotr Buła and Bartosz Niedzielski

Routledge
Taylor & Francis Group
LONDON AND NEW YORK

First published 2022
by Routledge
2 Park Square, Milton Park, Abingdon, Oxon OX14 4RN

and by Routledge
605 Third Avenue, New York, NY 10158

Routledge is an imprint of the Taylor & Francis Group, an informa business

British Library Cataloguing-in-Publication Data
A catalogue record for this book is available from the British Library

Library of Congress Cataloging-in-Publication Data
A catalog record has been requested for this book

ISBN: 978-1-032-02582-7 (hbk)
ISBN: 978-1-032-02583-4 (pbk)
ISBN: 978-1-003-18402-7 (ebk)

DOI: 10.4324/9781003184027

Typeset in Times New Roman
by Deanta Global Publishing Services, Chennai, India

Contents

Tables

Figures

Preface

Those who have never studied the artificial intelligence domain and have learned about its existence from media will be surprised that this concept, despite its present popularity, is more than 70 years old. It is generally understood that everything presently associated with artificial intelligence originated with the British mathematician and cryptologist Alan Turing, author of the famous test which, if passed, allowed calling a machine "intelligent". Today, Turing is regarded as the creator of artificial intelligence and contemporary information technology. To show appreciation for his scientific merits both to the world and the UK, the Bank of England has announced that Turing's image will be the face of a new GBP 50 banknote, which came into circulation in June 2021. Although a lot of theoretical and methodological solutions applied in artificial intelligence date back to distant times, a question arises as to why this field has become so popular today and why humanity attaches such great importance to it. The answer to this question, contrary to expectations, turns out to be quite simple, as important progress has been made over the last decade in computational power (see Tables 2.1 and 2.3), access to data and the scale of their growth currently counted in dozens of zettabytes (see Figure 4.4), as well as in the development of algorithmics. As a consequence, newly created evolutionary algorithms, error backpropagation algorithms, quantum algorithms or predictive algorithms are presently broadly applied in wide-ranging domains of life, from medicine, education, through science, industry, power generation, transport, mass media, administration, management, safety, business services, to agriculture, the natural environment or mining and fishery. In other words, elements of artificial intelligence have been permanently introduced into our lives, changing them in previously unknown and revolutionary ways. All indicates that this is just the beginning of a long path of structural changes, the range of which will encompass economies, societies and perhaps also religions. In fact, omnipresent development, e.g. of sensor and detector technologies may, in the near future, contribute to a spectacular development of electromobility, which will change forever not only the automotive market, but the petrochemical industry worldwide. Thereby, it is certain that changes will come, but it remains difficult to predict the force and scale with which they will redefine life on Earth.

A lot of opportunities and related challenges are faced today by many entities, including enterprises, which are the heart of the global economy. One such challenge, probably the most important one, is the organization's need to adjust to its changing environment. It should be noted that humanity, by contributing to the development of new technologies, one of which is artificial intelligence, has developed a business environment, previously unknown to organizations, to which they must now adapt and for which they will be forced to change, if they want to survive in the market. In other words, the artificial intelligence era will contribute to the **synanthropization or the organization** – the initiation of a process, in which entities will adapt to conditions created by human activities. In this context, adaptive processes in organizations will encompass e.g. organizational structures, management models, action strategies, work posts, inspection and supervision activities, internal audit, work organization and cooperation with business partners. Transformation will also affect the qualifications that managerial staff will need to possess in order to effectively manage the organization in the artificial intelligence era. The same will apply to employees, the employment of whom will be primarily determined by their cognitive abilities and meta-skills. The world of artificial intelligence and related technologies will result in data collection becoming the resource that all organizations will solicit most. On the other hand, the quality of data and data processing skills will become the determinants of the organization's market competitiveness.

Owing to the fact that the matters related to organization management in the artificial intelligence era lack a uniform framework in the literature, this book adopts a relatively universal approach. It is equipped not only with a wealth of definitions and terms directly or indirectly related to Industry 4.0 and artificial intelligence areas but also practical examples and guidelines for deepening and developing this technology in the field of management. In addition, the prognostic perspective that has been applied in each chapter in this book, in the authors' opinion, at least partially reduces the lack of confidence about the future of organizational functioning in the artificial intelligence era.

As the book presents a new and holistic approach to the methods, techniques, strategies and styles of organization management in an environment of highly advanced and innovative technologies, it may be useful for a wide range of recipients. Therefore, it can be a source of knowledge for students (on different study majors, not necessarily related to management), academic teachers, researchers and scientists and the broadly understood world of business, represented by entrepreneurs, managers or directors.

The book consists of four chapters, preceded by the preface and concluded by a summary. It has been equipped with tables and drawings that graphically supplement the problems and concepts being discussed. Furthermore, according to the Latin maxim *verba docent, example trahunt* (words teach, examples attract), the theoretical issues described in the book are supported by practical examples. The bibliography contains all source materials that have been utilized, entirely consisting of English language sources, which can become an additional inspiration for those readers who want to deepen their knowledge about the particular elements comprising the technologies forming artificial intelligence.

Chapter 1 introduces readers to the origins and development of Industry 4.0. The definitions, classifications and criteria related to the development of all global industrial revolutions cited in this chapter allow the reader not only to examine this topic, but also to individually evaluate its economic potential. In consequence – at the end of the chapter – readers will possess information about challenges and opportunities for the organization and the global economy that result from periods of discontinuous economic development.

Chapter 2 presents the stages of artificial intelligence evolution and the ways AI impacts economic reality. Readers have an opportunity to learn how life will function at the interaction of man–machine–work in the postmodern era. This chapter also contains a description of the development of Artificial Intelligence 2.0, and is concluded by investigations, supported by examples, into the application of artificial intelligence in different sectors of the economy.

Chapter 3 is fully devoted to the problems related to the functioning of organizations in the artificial intelligence era. Readers will gain knowledge about how the environment of artificial intelligence development affects the organization and vice versa, whether and how the present paradigms in management science will change, or how to adopt artificial intelligence-based solutions in an organization. Moreover, the chapter describes in detail a new type of organization, which will emerge across the globe due to the impact of artificial intelligence on organizations and the business environment.

Chapter 4 provides a detailed overview, at the global level, of the readiness of national artificial intelligence development strategies until 2030. The digital technology development strategies presented in the chapter, of the United States, China, the European Union, Brazil and Africa, introduce the reader to the world of tasks, actions, projects, programs and adaptation processes that are focused on stimulating the development of not only artificial intelligence, but innovation in general.

Acknowledgments

For the sake of brevity, we would like to acknowledge those who have had the greatest impact on our book. We want to emphasize that it would not have been written without the organizational, intellectual and financial assistance of several individuals and organizations. First, we would like to extend our thanks to our Alma Mater – Cracow University of Economics – for tremendous help and financial support. During our work, we experienced many great things from the university authorities, which we will always remember. Our sincere thanks also go to Mrs Anna Chrabąszcz – who proofread the text – for her kind advice, numerous valuable suggestions and for giving us ample opportunity to discuss editorial matters relevant to this project. As authors, we would like to appreciate the contribution of Routledge and its great staff under the direction of Guy Loft, who provided us with invaluable help in organizational and logistical matters, and who played an inspiring role in developing the book's final concept. In our opinion, its team paved the way for books like this one to have a chance of succeeding on an international, and maybe even global scale. Finally, we sincerely thank our loved ones for their constant encouragement and support during the writing of this book.

Piotr Buła and Bartosz Niedzielski

1 Industrial revolution – from Industry 1.0 to Industry 4.0

1.1 Genesis and development of Industry 4.0

From the evolutionary perspective, the development of Industry 4.0 started at the turn of the 18th and 19th centuries, with the transition from craft and manufacture production to mechanized factory production, which became the **First Industrial Revolution (Industrial Revolution 1.0)**. A pioneer of those early transformations was James Watt, a Scottish engineer and inventor from Glasgow, who, in the winter of 1763, received a lucrative, though difficult to complete order regarding improvements in one of the first steam pumps in the UK (Pottin & Dietz, 2018). As it turned out later, for Watt the task became the *idée fixe*, which did not leave him in subsequent years. The inventor received help from a friendly plumber, whose involvement and – for those times – primitive tools resulted in the design of the steam engine, which was the device's central drive unit. Watt's achievement, which was an improvement on the atmospheric steam engine developed by Thomas Newcomen,[1] was thereby regarded as a breakthrough in industrial technology and proclaimed a worldwide industrial revolution. In recognition of his achievement, in 1769 Watt was awarded his first patent by the King of England.

In the context of the above, it should be noted that the First Industrial Revolution, beginning around 1760 and ending around 1840, was and is an important part in the world's economic history, which paved the way for its future development. It began an era of mechanization and the use of a number of (at the time) innovative technical inventions, primarily for the production of energy. The changes that occurred at that time also revolutionized people's thinking about the workplace and methods of performing work. With mechanization, it was possible to produce the same things in factories eight times faster than before. As a result, for the first time in the world's history the individual and his/her "costly" work were being substituted by steam machines driven by cheap coal. From the economic point of view, this substitution led to reductions in the earlier costs of production and an almost exponential growth in work efficiency, which was reflected in related profits. Work automation related to the application of the steam machine in the mining industry, or later in textiles, was the largest breakthrough in the history of production. Importantly, the achieved effect was further strengthened by the discoveries that humanity experienced at the beginning of the 19th century, primarily

DOI: 10.4324/9781003184027-1

James Neilson's[2] "hot blast" or George Stephenson's[3] steam locomotive. The first of these inventions contributed to a significant reduction in the cost of fuel in metallurgical furnaces, while the second enabled the transportation of cargo across substantial distances in less time. In consequence, civilizational development at the onset of the 19th century became even more dynamic. To a significant extent, which is worth emphasizing, it was a result of efforts of talented engineers, chemists, physicists or technologists, rather than an accident or a gift from the gods.

The term "industrial revolution" was used again in 1936 by the French sociologist and psychologist Georges Friedmann to describe the changes that were taking place in Europe and in the United States during the first half of the 19th century, related to the effects of mass production, which utilized assembly lines, division of labor, development of the human being and that of entire societies.[4] It is commonly accepted in literature that the **Second Industrial Revolution (Industrial Revolution 2.0)** falls in the period 1870–1914. This means that, after one hundred years from the beginning of the First Industrial Revolution, the world and humanity had to face another one, this time characterized by even greater upgrades and challenges. The greatest innovations connected with the Second Industrial Revolution era, which strongly affected the dynamics of industrial development at that time, were directly linked to two new energy sources: electricity (electric motor) and oil and natural gas (internal combustion engine). With them, the industrial world witnessed a sudden transition from conventional production methods to more innovative ones, based on new technologies, which changed the earlier processes of manufacturing and processing goods that took place in the majority of British and US factories. However, the changes, important from the point of view of technology and innovation, were taking place not only in industry, but also in communications or transportation. In the case of communications a considerable role for human development and the world was played initially by the telegraph,[5] which revolutionized communication systems and allowed people to communicate remotely and then by the telephone,[6] the forefather of the smartphone, which is now considered the foundation of contemporary communication systems. In transportation, groundbreaking for that era and later also the world's further history, were discoveries by US aviation pioneers, the Wright brothers.[7] It is thanks to their talent that the airplane became a new means of transport, and distance ceased to be of significance. In addition, the principles of mechanics and steering in aviation that they developed remain the standard of aircraft design to this day. The American industrialist Henry Ford also had an invaluable contribution to the development of transport at that time. The first prototype of the car he built in 1896 marked the beginning of the development of the automotive sector, which changed forever people's thinking about transport, distances and time. Significantly from the point of view of work organization, Ford performed a true revolution by introducing a moving assembly line to his factories, and forever changed the layout of production plants, shift-based work systems, thinking about cost and profits in companies and occupational safety.

The Second Industrial Revolution, unlike the first one, was primarily characterized by the fact that it was supported, to a large extent, by an appropriate scientific base, which in practice allowed for better and more effective use of (previously known) processes and made technology more effective (utile) (Mokyr & Strotz, 2000). In addition, it changed the world's thinking about organization of production, mainly due to a surge in industrial efficiency and the phenomenon of economies of scale. The standard of living was also improving gradually, although not very significantly. However, as noticed by Mokyr and Strotz (2000), technological leadership was still monopolized at the time by the industrialized Western world.

An opinion can be proposed that, while the First Industrial Revolution prepared the ground for the development of the Second Industrial Revolution, the Second Industrial Revolution, in particular in the area of skillful use of knowledge and technology, prepared a stable ground for the development of the **Third Industrial Revolution (Industrial Revolution 3.0)** (see Figure 1.1). It is commonly assumed in the literature that it lasted from 1969 to 2000. However, for clarity of analysis, this period can be divided into two sub-periods: the first one from 1969 to 1989 and the second one from 1990 to 2000. The first sub-period was distinguished by the introduction of the first programmable logical controllers[8] (earlier: sequential logical controllers), which were in fact microprocessor devices intended to control the work of machines or other technological devices, including personal computers and production lines. Thanks to their application, in 1987 computers could start "cooperating" with the first professional office applications, which irreversibly revolutionized organization management methods. The second of the listed sub-periods covers the years of dynamic development of the Internet and the growing digitization of work, which, through their influence, determined new paradigms of life for individuals and entire societies. As a result, Industrial Revolution 3.0 created millions of new workplaces and paved the way for the development of the sustainable global economy of the 21st century, based on renewable energy resources. Therefore, the whole "strategy" of the Third Industrial Revolution, in the opinion of Rifkin (2012), is based on five pillars, inseparably inter-related, and is connected with:

- first – shifting to renewable energy,[9]
- second – transformation of available buildings on each continent into micro power plants, which are to collect scattered renewable energy,
- third – implementation of a technology for intermittent energy storage,
- fourth – use of IT and online technologies to convert power transmission and electric lines into the so-called energy internet,
- and fifth – transitioning the whole transport fleet to electrically propelled vehicles, which can buy and sell this "fuel" within an intelligent, continental and interactive energy grid.

It should be noted that the Third Industrial Revolution was organized around renewable energy, fairly scattered, which, when gradually collected and "computerized" using continental "green" electric energy grids, is to support the sustainable development of the economies in the 21st century.

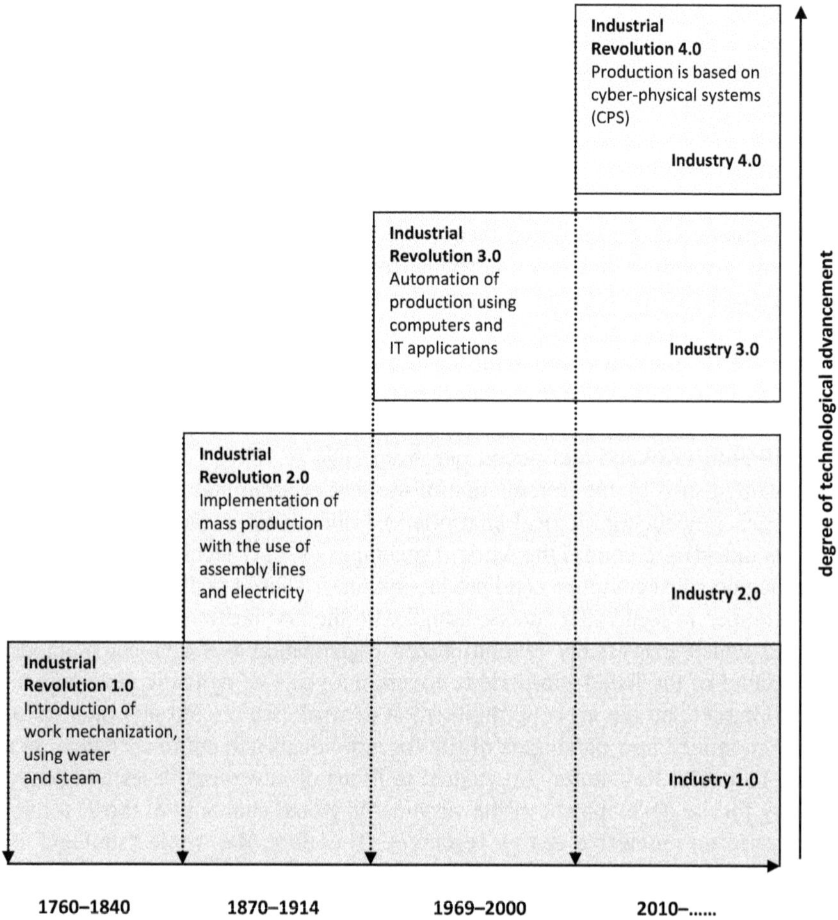

Figure 1.1 From Industry 1.0 to Industry 4.0 – stages of evolution. Source: Study based on Deloitte (2015).

At present, economic development and the related qualitative changes progress so rapidly that, at the onset of the 21st century, humanity nearly overlooked the moment of transition to the next, **Fourth Industrial Revolution (Industrial Revolution 4.0)**. To better comprehend the pace of current changes, it is enough to notice that within the last 50 years humanity has twice experienced industrial revolutions, while earlier it needed more than 150 (see Figure 1.1). This means that the pace of change is presently more than double that of the early 20th century. While the Third Industrial Revolution was centered on automation of machines and simple production processes, supported by online technology, the fourth revolution brings a systemic digital transformation, encompassing all fixed assets and a deep integration with business partners having similar values within the combined service network, known as digital ecosystems.[10] In other words, the

Fourth Industrial Revolution will be characterized, above all, by growing digitization and a deep correlation of products, services, values and business models within particular sectors and areas of the economy. In this context, Pottin and Dietz (2018) observe that the goals of the Fourth Industrial Revolution – especially in the area of production – will focus upon:

- introducing smart machines to enterprises, which will fully control production processes on their own,
- combining different production methods with state-of-the-art IT and communication technologies with digital support of systems which will significantly enable independent management of manufacturing processes,
- implementing smart processes for monitoring and making management decisions in enterprises, which will allow activities to be controlled and optimized in organizations, in close-to-real time,
- using smart machines in enterprises, which may communicate with one another, inform each interested party about defects in the production process, and create a list of inventory materials necessary for the production process.

Bearing in mind the above, it must be concluded that the concept of the Fourth Industrial Revolution will permanently change the operating model of enterprises both in industry and services. In practice, the present production and services management processes will be significantly transformed. The generation and exchange of huge data volumes by numerous cyberphysical systems will not only allow us to monitor the current status of production and service processes, but above all will create better possibilities for forecasting their behavior in the future, both in terms of qualitative and quantitative parameters. In this way, production and provision of services will improve, from the point of view of time and production factors. These circumstances will not be without effects on humanity and the earlier role people served in the organization, which now will have to change dramatically. The Fourth Industrial Revolution, discussed in detail further in this book, will require from people completely new skills and capabilities, which, to a significant extent, will be concerned with advanced adaptability to the quickly changing reality, creative problem-solving in combination with the skills of operating modern digital equipment or well developed emotional intelligence.

To sum up, it should be emphasized that, apart from the general trends that have been outlined in this chapter with reference to the Fourth Industrial Revolution, its driving forces will continue to be the following (PwC, 2016):

- first – **digital transformation and the continuing process of horizontal and vertical integration of value chains**. This means that one of the forces of the Fourth Industrial Revolution is the ability to horizontally transform and integrate processes across the entire organization, from product purchase and design, through production, logistics, to services. On the other hand, when it comes to vertical integration, it goes beyond the area of the company's internal actions and reaches out to suppliers and customers, at the same time encompassing all key partners in the value chain. This type of integration is based on new digital technologies enabling identification and tracking as well as integrated real-time task planning and performance,

- second – **digitization of the product range and services using state-of-the-art technologies**. The digitization of products is concerned with the expansion of existing products, or their whole portfolio, by equipping them with smart sensors or communication equipment, which can later be used along with data analysis devices. By integration of new data collection methods and data analysis, companies are able to generate additional information for further product improvement, to fulfill rapidly growing expectations of end customers,
- third – **digitization of business models and access to customers**. With digitization of business models, companies are able to expand their product lines by sharing additional data analysis services with their customers, or creating integrated digital platforms. In addition, it focuses on optimized interaction with the client. An important element in the model is the offering of specific digital products and services within a particular digital ecosystem.[11]

To end this section, which reviews industrial revolutions that humanity has experienced over the last 250 years, it can be argued that the "achievements" of each of them were directly proportional to the level of usefulness of the knowledge at the time when the revolution occurred. Therefore, the growing usefulness of knowledge, taking place since 1760 (see Figure 1.1), manifesting itself in increasingly effective methods of using it to create new technologies, has made it the crucial element in the 21st century, shaping the pace of economic development of the world and individual nations. This rule was already noticed by Kuznets (1965), who argued more than 50 years ago that economic growth is determined first of all by the level of useful knowledge.

1.2 Industry 4.0 – definition-based perspective

Industry 4.0 is the term used in reference to the Fourth Industrial Revolution. For several years this topic has raised notable interest of both management practitioners and theoreticians of management. The attention of the former focuses, first of all, on financial success from the goods that are offered by Industry 4.0, while the latter observe, and also measure and analyze this phenomenon and examine how this industrial revolution will redefine the present organization management models. It is thus highly probable that each of us has heard about Industry 4.0 at least once; however not everybody has a clear or well researched notion of it. Therefore, a comprehensive analysis will be undertaken in this chapter regarding the meaning and the origins of the term Industry 4.0.

The term Industry 4.0 (German *Industrie 4.0*) was coined for the first time in public space in 2011, during the annual Hanover industrial fair ("Hannover Messe"), considered the largest industrial exhibition today. The use of this concept was directly related to an initiative of some representatives of the German business community, politics, but also science, to promote stronger competitiveness of the German industry in the face of quickly catching-up competitors from China.[12] The concept appealed so much to representatives of the German government that they decided to make Industry 4.0 one of the key elements in Germany's new research and technological innovation policy. As a result, details related to the development of German *Industrie 4.0*, including Germany as the global leader in technological innovation, were included in a document issued by the Federal Ministry of Education and Research, entitled "The High-Tech Strategy 2020 for Germany".[13] Apart from the term Industry 4.0, applied to describe phenomena related to the development of the Fourth Industrial Revolution, there are also other synonyms used in the literature, including: "Industry of the Future", "Cyber-Physical Systems Era" (CPSs Era), "Production of the Future", "Intelligent Manufacturing Systems" (IMSs) or 4IR (Fourth Industrial Revolution). We can often also come across the term, actually quite trivial, "Smart Factory". However, in the United States or generally in the English language-speaking countries, the following terms are more often used for Industry 4.0: "Internet of Things" (IoT), "Internet of Everything" (IoE), or "Industrial Internet of Things" (IIoT). Being aware of the wealth of terms used to describe the current industrial revolution available in the subject literature, it should be noted that the most frequently found term, not only in bibliometric databases, but generally, is Industry 4.0.

In the broad meaning, it is defined as the next development stage of the organization and value chain management in the manufacturing industry. Industry 4.0 is defined in a similar way by Hermann, Pentek and Otto (2016), who laconically state[14] that this is a collective term for the technology and the concept of value chain organization. An interesting definition is presented by experts from Siemens, who relate Industry 4.0 directly to automation, processing and exchange of large amounts of data by technologically advanced tools, within the so-called cyberphysical systems. In practice, this is reflected in production digitization, where technological devices and systems communicate online, thereby ensuring the possibility to obtain and analyze large amounts of production data (Siemens, 2017). Liffler and Tschiesner (2013) present a similar position as the experts from Siemens (2017), yet paying attention to the fact that machines, devices or systems being connected with each other have an opportunity, in a digitized production environment, not only to analyze but also to mutually control data. This makes it possible for example to forecast failures of equipment, automatically launch maintenance processes or independently organize necessary logistics, as a reaction to unusual changes in their operations. An interesting, although clearly descriptive light on the term Industry 4.0 has also been cast by Wong et al. (2016), claiming that its primary idea focuses first of all on the use of constantly emerging information technologies to implement IoT-related concepts. In consequence, in their opinion, what is happening is a deep integration of both business and engineering processes, which results in the presence of integrated, yet highly customized manufacturing, characterized by high flexibility, efficiency, environmental sustainability, top quality and low cost. Therefore, even putting aside the presently existing methods of process management or control, it can be concluded that Industry 4.0 is directly associated with the growing flexibility of industrial manufacturing or services and their higher competitiveness level as compared to other products on the market.

In the narrow perspective we can define Industry 4.0 as a digital transformation of manufacturing, utilizing modern technologies such as Big Data (large data collections), IoT or augmented reality (AR) in order to integrate factories, processes for highly customized and low-cost manufacturing. In his proposed definition of Industry 4.0, Anderl (2014) additionally mentions the possibilities that this concept offers in the context of taking advantage of cyberphysical systems (CPS) for technical communication capabilities between various devices, thereby creating so-called intelligent systems.

In the context of the above, despite the fact that both broad and narrow perspectives of the term Industry 4.0 put emphasis on slightly different aspects of this phenomenon, what is unquestionably the common element between them is the notion of digitization of both systems and the whole production environment, ubiquitously repeated in the concept definitions. In this way, all components and crucial technologies of Industry 4.0 (see Table 1.1), regardless of location and positioning, can mutually communicate with one another and act autonomously, which proves their innovative nature. The above-mentioned definitions of the term Industry 4.0 are only a small part of what we can currently find in the literature devoted to this topic. In spite of the wealth of terms, the definitions differ from one another, just like the interpretations concerning the phenomenon itself

Table 1.1 Industry 4.0 – basic technologies and concepts

Group	*Technologies and concepts*
Smart factories	Cyber-Physical Systems (CPS) Embedded Systems (ES) Radio-Frequency Identification (RFID) Internet of Things (IoT) Internet of Services (IoS) Automation Modularization Additive Manufacturing (AM) Product Lifecycle Management (PLM) Robotics Human–Computer Interaction (HCI)
Simulation and modeling	Simulation tools and models Augmented Reality (AR) Virtual Reality (VR) Mixed Reality (MR)
Digitalization and virtualization	Cloud Computing Big Data Mobile Computing Social Media Digitalization

Source: Study based on Oesterreich and Teuteberg (2016).

and the processes related to the Fourth Industrial Revolution. Therefore, one cannot be surprised by the fact that, so far, no uniform definition of Industry 4.0 has been developed in the literature that would be commonly accepted by all circles interested in these issues. Furthermore, the argumentation behind adopting one or another definition of Industry 4.0 for common use often does not include any substantive assessments, or any criteria that the authors had in mind when creating the concept.

From a holistic, but also a scientific point of view, apart from the definitions presented earlier, of crucial importance for the concept of Industry 4.0 are the component technologies and solutions that comprise it (see Table 1.1). All together, and each separately, comprise a certain type of a system of mutual linkages and digital interdependencies, thereby creating an environment for the functioning of Industry 4.0 (see Figure 1.2). Importantly, the epicenter of this environment is formed by the smart factory of the future, with a modular design, based on cyberphysical systems. Thanks to them and respective software, smart communication (including automatic coordination) takes place continuously between the elements forming the smart factory and the smart factory and the surrounding environment. An important component of this environment is the smart

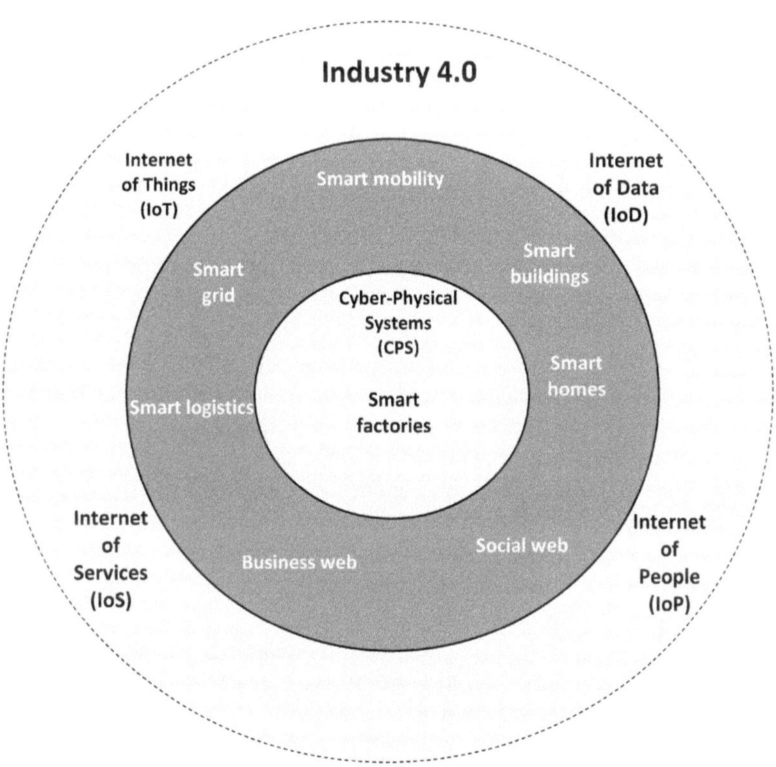

Figure 1.2 The environment of Industry 4.0. Source: Study based on Deloitte (2015).

infrastructure in the form of smart mobility, smart transmission network, smart transport or smart buildings (see Figure 1.2). An important role is also played by business network linkages with various types of global social media portals, such as Facebook,[15] YouTube, Instagram, Pinterest, Weibo or Twitter, which increasingly often dominate the digital transformation of societies towards Industry 4.0. Therefore, the changes that are taking place in this area are already inevitable and the trend cannot be stopped. In the end, this process is strongly stimulated by the development not only of the Internet of Things or data, but the internet of everything[16] (including people, processes, data and things).

Having knowledge about what Industry 4.0 is and what technologies and concepts create its environment, it is worth asking another question, this time regarding the key characteristics, including those of the factory or system, which are typical for Industry 4.0. In other words, the point is to define those common attributes that will always be identified with the technology and concepts of the Fourth Industrial Revolution. In this regard there is full consent in the subject literature – which is not a common occurrence. A significant majority of the authors (Maslarić et al., 2016; Smit et al., 2016) argue that the major features distinguishing Industry 4.0 are centered on:

- **interoperability**[17] – in general it means the possible comprehensive cooperation of different, often also separate, "elements" to pursue agreed goals, beneficial for all parties. In the context of Industry 4.0, the aim is to combine into a network and ensure mutual communication of smart factories or people through IoT and IoS. In practice, the collective communication of facilities, machines, devices or people taking place online and through cyberphysical systems determines whether, in the context of Industry 4.0, we are actually dealing with *smart factory* or only with *factory*,
- **virtualization** – is in fact the use of particular software to build an abstraction of possessed resources. Hence, in the area of Industry 4.0, virtualization comes down to the possibility of combining cyberphysical systems with virtual models and simulations. CPS must therefore have the "ability" to simulate and create copies of the real world. It is on the basis of virtualization that there is a possibility to create a virtual copy of a smart factory, as a result of combining data from sensors with virtual models of various types of things,
- **decentralization** – essentially, it is about the method of making decisions and managing being performed independently and simultaneously in separate subsystems. Simply speaking, it is about the cyberphysical systems' ability to work independently. Such an approach creates a new area for the preparation of non-standard products and solving "unusual" problems, making the manufacturing environment more flexible and productive. On the other hand, in the case of any conflicts related to the accomplishment of common goals, the problem is raised to a higher level in the system,
- **real-time capability** – applies to the ability of devices or systems to immediately react to key information collected automatically from other machines. Adaptation to real-time requirements is the foundation for each type of

communication, decision-making or systems management in the real world. From the point of view of future manufacturing, a smart factory must hence have the ability to collect and analyze data in real time. In fact, decisions are made on this basis and they must be in line with the objectives pursued by the organization. A similar situation is the case for the identification of defects or hazards that should be quickly "captured" in the system or device, and then transferred to other operating objects, in order to fix or neutralize them. Such approach to production management probably should be conducive to its flexibility and optimization,

- **service orientation** – which is directly related to customer-oriented production. From the point of view of the Industry of the Future, products created for customers reflect their tastes or preferences that have been identified as a result of connecting humans with intelligent facilities and partner networks via the Internet. In this context, it can be concluded that, with the Internet of Services, a "center of global consumer preferences" is created,
- **modularity** – systems connected to the Industry of the Future should as far as possible be characterized by modularity, in order to ensure that there is a possibility to quickly reconstruct them if the need arises. In practice, the point is to ensure that smart factories can adapt flexibly to dynamically changing market requirements, trends or the environment they operate in, e.g. by replacing or expanding the selected module. In the past, the "inborn" lack of flexibility of many organizations made adaptation processes take long months and often even years, which not only generated additional costs, but also reduced their market competitiveness.

For many managers and business owners, the characteristics of Industry 4.0 presented above can pose as guidelines when designing their own smart factories of the future. These are prerequisites, but they are unfortunately insufficient for such an object to function effectively in the era of cyberphysical systems. A whole range of additional actions need to be undertaken, in the areas of standardization of systems, platforms or connections, work organization, design of modern business models, securing technological knowledge against competitor actions and in areas related to human resources, research and development or intellectual property.

To sum up this section, it should be emphasized that the concept of Industry 4.0, as revealed in the definitions quoted above, shows significant differentiation in relation to traditional technological forms which exist to this day in manufacturing or service areas. These differences are especially manifested in relation to (Maslarić et al., 2016):

- **products** – which are more personalized, and the production of which is optimized and low-cost,
- **processes** – which, based on network solutions, eliminate barriers regarding knowledge and investment as well as serving the enhanced development of small and medium enterprises,

- **business models** – which presently no longer eliminate small companies from the battle for global markets (small does not mean weak),
- **competitors** – who have access to each customer market in the world,
- **skills** – which have evolved towards competences of the future, namely meta-skills,[18] which will be discussed further in this book,
- **the globalization process** – which has created previously unknown opportunities for the global presence of "everything".

Bearing in mind the technologies, state-of-the-art concepts and solutions, cyber-physical systems or finally the Internet itself, all of which directly determine the driving force of the Fourth Industrial Revolution, a question arises about the economic potential of Industry 4.0. The answer to this question is neither easy nor unambiguous.

1.3 Industry 4.0 – economic potential of the Fourth Industrial Revolution

Prediction, especially in relation to economic processes, is extremely difficult and bears high levels of uncertainty. This results mainly from the fact that the prediction process consists of a high number of factors, both internal and external, which when additionally exhibiting high variability over time, disturb the image of the future being modeled. Bearing in mind these difficulties, estimation of the economic potential of the Fourth Industrial Revolution seems to be a risky task, especially when in the case of Industry 4.0 we are not dealing with one, but several technological innovations. Furthermore, as correctly pointed out by Schröder (2017), some of these technologies, although at an advanced stage of development, still need time to reach the market in mature form. Moreover, different stages of these devices' technological maturity make it difficult to determine the time that is necessary for them to enter into commercial use. In turn, this means no possibility to predict when humanity will be able to reap the "fruits" of their use. However, based on the assumptions made by some authors in their works on the potential of 4IR, an attempt can be made to define it, at least in general. Initially it should be pointed out that each industrial revolution contains its own economic potential. The Fourth Industrial Revolution is no different, as it undoubtedly has the potential to reshape the global economy, based on digitized and low-cost manufacturing. This positive image of the potential in Industry 4.0 is in fact noticed by most dealing with these problems on a daily basis. In this context, a question arises: how to fully use this potential for the benefit of as many people worldwide as possible? Certainly this task will require both broad international cooperation and large financial outlays. As an example, it is worth referring to the results of research that were published as early as 2014 by Roland Berger[19] in a report entitled *Industry 4.0. The new industrial revolution. How Europe will succeed* (Blanche et al., 2014). The study argues that if Europe wants to play a leading role in Industry 4.0, it has to allocate annually EUR 90 billion for the next 15 years specifically for this purpose. This means that until 2030 Europe will need EUR

1.35 trillion to utilize the economic potential of Industry 4.0. In this context, bearing in mind the macroeconomic situation of some European economies, it may turn out that they are not able to sustain excessively high budgetary expenses on the development of this industry, or that this burden may lead them into a spiral of debt. Such a pessimistic scenario would mean increased budget deficits in these countries, and possibly expose them to sanctions imposed by the authorities of the European Union (EU), especially via the excessive deficit procedure.[20]

Gloomy scenarios aside, it should be expressly emphasized that technological innovations related to the development of Industry 4.0 will be the driving forces behind the growth of any economy in the nearest 15–20 years. In practice, this will be reflected in the pace of its economic development and GDP/per capita. In addition, the new era of Industry 4.0 will leave a mark on all sectors and industries, causing a structural transformation in the world economy, the effect of which will be the formation of a new work division paradigm that will particularly affect the economies of developing countries. In other words, we will witness a deep transformation not only of how we will be working, but also how we will be living and cooperating with each other. From the microeconomic point of view, the economic potential of Industry 4.0 will still be used mostly to make production processes flexible together with their increasing level of digitization, which in the final analysis is to support the design of low cost manufacturing. The possibilities offered by Industry 4.0, especially from the point of view of cost reduction, are best illustrated by the fact that in 1994 the annual storage cost of 1GB of data was USD 10 000, while in 2016 it was just USD 0.03 (Schwab, 2016). Moreover, currently it is estimated that intelligent automation being part of smart factories already allows for the total time of machine standstill to be reduced by 30–50 percent, decreasing costs on average by 20 percent. Here it is necessary to add that outages in factories are today one of the most urgent challenges related to the production process. Currently it is estimated that one minute of standstill may cost a vehicle manufacturer as much as USD 22 000, and, interestingly enough, the average cost of unplanned downtimes in industry e.g. the chemical and petrochemical industries, is annually estimated at as much as USD 20 billion (Flex International Ltd., 2019).

From the technological point of view, in the context of intelligent automation the most important role will perhaps be played by cyberphysical systems (CPS) that are at the core of the Industry 4.0 environment (see Figure 1.2). Their invaluable advantage is that they strictly integrate together various systems in all scales and at all levels. CPS integrate both calculations and physical processes. Moreover, with built-in systems and computer networks, they may be able to communicate with other devices, and in this way can control their operation. Apart from that, they have feedback transmission "abilities" e.g. about the impact of physical processes on calculations and the impact of calculations on physical processes. In practice, the consolidation of all these components makes it possible to efficiently manage and monitor the previously designed system. Still, the potential present within CP systems must be further analyzed and, most importantly, developed. Science is to play a crucial role in this process, through its contribution to the further development of technological innovation, and will therefore effectively support the vision of CPS extension. In the nearest future, science will be the determinant of economy competitiveness on the global market of products and services. Therefore, from the point of view of the state, it is crucial to create scientific and technological foundations for the development of CPS. The resulting benefits will probably be significant, including unprecedented breakthroughs in science and engineering. Their emergence, bearing in mind the omnipresence of technology, is only a matter of time, and it will not remain without effect on a substantial part of the world's economies. Thus, CPS is a technology that presently not only offers a lot of opportunities to the states, in terms of economic self-development, but also "requires" that still valid challenges be addressed, which are concerned with (Rajkumar et al., 2010):

- uninterrupted generation and distribution of electric power in the world,[21]
- further growth of efficiency and sustainable development at all stages of the value chain in agriculture (see European Commission, 2016),
- safe and quick evacuation in response to natural disasters or those caused by human activities,
- access to world class medicine, including the most advanced therapy methods and techniques regardless of the place of residence,
- elimination of mortal accidents and limitation of road traffic jams and delays,
- design of more energy-efficient buildings and cities,
- creation of more modern preventive maintenance methods for **physical critical infrastructure**,[22]
- development of self-repairing CPS systems, using one application.

The challenges presented do not exhaust the list of all that CPS technology will have to face. However, it is certain that most of them will concentrate on a permanent pursuit of increasing the degree of reliability and safety of operation of modern systems, processes or equipment. An important role will also be played by the matters related to limiting consumption of resources, especially limited ones. The same will apply to improvements in the efficiency of particular processes, in which any elements unable to add value will be automatically eliminated or modified. In practice, as we can see already, a strong emphasis will be put on the construction of autonomous vehicles, including aircraft and trains that will be controlled solely by autopilot. This implies that, in the case of a smart car, the drive will be collision-free, and the driver will avoid the need to have a driver's license, and while driving will be able to read a book, hold a teleconference, answer emails or, simply speaking, "take a nap". As an example, at this point it is just worth mentioning that for over two years such companies as Google, Apple or Uber have been testing, mostly in the United States, their autonomous cars, which, as their designers anticipate, can go into public use as early as in 2021 or 2022. Autonomous cars from Google have driven more than 1.5 million km, not causing any accident or even a fender-bender. Until recently they were tested mostly on US highways, and then Google decided to transfer them to cities, including Mountain View, California. With the tests taking place there and continuous modifications, the cars can already detect pedestrians and other vehicles, including those driving out from unlit streets or those with poor visibility. Furthermore, with real-time road scanning, autopilot-equipped cars developed by engineers from Google are able to detect traffic problems related to roadworks, independently identify an emergency lane for temporary parking, pass by cars parked on the road, move from an intersection at the right time, both with the light signaling system both on and off, recognize that a cyclist extending a hand right or left wants to complete a turning maneuver, or stop in front of a vehicle standing in a traffic jam. Therefore, it should be expected that "driverless cars" will become a significant link in smart transport, which will contribute to minimization, and perhaps complete elimination of traffic jams in the future. It is beyond doubt that a great importance will be attached to the building of **smart cities,**[23] a component of which may be created by smart transport, including smart cars. Currently, in many cities worldwide, among other issues, public safety problems are solved using smart CCTV cameras.[24] As a result, respective emergency services can quickly react to any deviant behaviors, inconsistent with the adopted standards of social coexistence, as recorded by CCTV cameras on municipal squares, streets or housing estates. Bearing this in mind, within CPS technology a problem to be solved is one connected with the common identification of persons committing acts of vandalism, who, often with obscured faces, make the identification process difficult for prosecution bodies. In part, this issue has already been solved for example in China. It turns out that in the face recognition segment, two Chinese companies Megvia (Face++) and SenseTime Group have developed a technological solution which, with the use of smart cameras, artificial intelligence and a database of 700 million photographs[25] of Chinese citizens, allows identification of faces of any persons (including those with obscured faces) who violate the law in public places or whose behavior is inconsistent with the principles of coexistence within the structure of Chinese society. As a result, this solution is increasingly used by the Chinese police across the whole country. With regard to smart cities being discussed here, it is also necessary to emphasize an issue related to designing buildings that are to consume less energy, heat and water in the future.[26] In the case of water, the main focus is on the whole system referred to as smart water, to be understood as the entire water and wastewater infrastructure which, if properly designed and managed, can guarantee that a valuable resource such as water will be used in cities in the most effective way. Therefore, the water management and distribution system in smart cities must be properly designed and cost-effective in the long run. Moreover, it should be equipped with options to monitor and connect with other systems, which are critical from the point of view of this good (e.g. with meteorological stations). In this situation, it is of key importance to develop and increase the functionalities, in particular the digital ones, of the currently possessed models of water supply or sanitary sewer grids that, when properly designed, will contribute to:

- increasing the potential resulting from smart water management in cities,
- greater optimization of the parameters in the entire water and sewage infrastructure,

- reducing the energy necessary for proper operation of the entire smart water system,
- quickly identifying any alarm situations including e.g. water leakages from the system.

In the context of the topic presented above, we should agree that in spite of the undoubtedly huge potential of Industry 4.0 in general, and CPS technology in particular, there is still a lot to do in this area. Probably some of the above-mentioned challenges related to cyberphysical systems can be accomplished faster, while humanity will be forced to wait for a solution to the other ones even a decade or more. In fact, everything will depend on the degree of utilizing the strong connection that has always existed between engineering and science, in designing and building smart systems, especially since cyberphysical systems comprise a high number of interconnected sensors and devices, which affect each other and the surrounding environment. As a result, the existence of a compound-complex system creates scientific and technical problems which are not easy to solve but are critical from the point of view of building the future, omnipresent CPS system. That is why a key matter for the future development of Industry 4.0 will be organizations' ability to use the potential they will have in the field of knowledge. Importantly, it must also be safely collected and stored, due to the sensitivity of the gathered information related to customers' data, for example. Such knowledge will accompany the further development of Industry 4.0, which will change the world as we know it. After all, manufacturing will to a significant extent be based on broadly understood digitization and organizations will fully subordinate the present processes, procedures, organizational culture or management styles to the rapidly changing needs of their customers. The Industry of the Future will therefore require significant mobilization of both funds and human resources, and utilization of its potential, not only economic, will also depend on thinking about:

- the role of humans and machines in the digitization era,
- attitudes, preparations and expectations of employees towards the Fourth Industrial Revolution
- use of the present and new knowledge for sustainable development of the world,
- impact of Industry 4.0 on work, organizations and the society,
- negative consequences related to the digital transformation, including newly created lifestyle diseases,
- impact of Industry 4.0 on the development of medicine and people's health,
- change of the present paradigms in the field of management,
- a fundamental change of the present lifestyle,
- (cyber) security for the world,
- impact of the virtual world on the real world.

To end the deliberations in this section, it is worth mentioning the potential being discussed here, not only in economic and social terms but also the scientific potential embedded in Industry 4.0. It is worth mentioning that the industrial revolution happening in front of our eyes and the related smart manufacturing, smart infrastructure or **smart management**,[27] form a relatively new research area, which inevitably creates new problems and challenges for science. Due to the pioneering nature and innovative character of some research problems, science will probably need much greater financial outlays than before, especially requiring governments presently to put particular emphasis on scientific research and innovation holding the promise of results that can be quickly commercialized, either in the form of patents, technologies, products or services. The strengthening of the scientific potential in the context of Industry 4.0 has to refer, importantly, not only to universities or state research institutes, but also to enterprises. That is why the competence centers for industry already operate in some countries, in particular highly developed countries, with the aim of increasing, through research and development, the innovation level of primarily the small and medium enterprise sector. In addition, increasingly often, at the national and international levels, we come across the idea of creating broad scientific and research platforms whose goal is cooperation and integration of the worlds of science, business and politics. Teams developed this way are working together on new solutions and inventions that can successfully be implemented in the 21st-century world. As a result, it should be expected that, along with the development of the Fourth Industrial Revolution, the present paradigm of running scientific research will be changed, in the sense that any knowledge will have to hold promise for creating a commercial product, technology or service. In fact, at most higher education institutions such an approach has so far only been more a subject of academic discussion than of real actions. In consequence, cooperation between higher education institutions and the world of business has come down only to creating a program of, mostly unpaid, student internships or arranging common study curricula.

1.4 Industry 4.0 – implementation barriers versus support conditions

Introducing the results of technological progress to an organization has always involved specific problems, because new technologies carry changes that often apply not only to mere organizations, but entire industries and sectors. Therefore, change, often a radical one, subjugates current production processes, methods and techniques of processing information or even management models and styles. All these factors, either together or each of them separately, affect the spheres of human activity, which leads in consequence to building a limitless network of relations and interdependencies between its forming elements. The final "product" of this process is a **cross-linked economy**, characterized by the speed of the changes taking place, a high competition level, extensive data communication networks and mass customization, which changes the contemporary cultural, business or consumption models. Owing to the fact that technological changes cannot be stopped or go unnoticed, we should adjust to them. In practice, this requires from organizations, both large and small, proper reactions to the dynamically changing economic reality. In fact, any under-appreciation of the change process may become the first step to the organization's collapse. This was the case for the Kodak Company, a legend on the photography market: the company's representatives' persistent ignoring of the technological revolution in the area of digital photography[28] to which the company had contributed[29] led in 2012, after 131 years of presence on the market, to Kodak's bankruptcy. At present, the number of organizations that approach technological, and, in consequence, market changes as disrespectfully as Kodak is rather small. In fact, among management staff the awareness of lagging "behind" enforces attitudes focused on innovation, deeper exploration of the market and its specific nature as well as better sensing of customer moods. Therefore, they also benefit more and more often from solutions offered in this area by Industry 4.0. However, full access to such technologies is not easy and often involves many "sacrifices" of an organizational, technical and financial nature. How an organization can overcome the existing barriers, and then implement Industry 4.0 solutions, depends on many factors. One of them is company size. In the case of large businesses where, due to the volume, manufacturing is often already automated and the processes optimized, the adaptation of 4IR applications seems to be much easier, both in terms of the costs and the technical solutions. Moreover, it is almost a standard in large companies that the processes of decision-making, supervision or circulation of documents are already fully digitized. When it comes to small and medium enterprises, the situation looks quite different. In many of them, a significant percentage of actions, processes or works is still performed manually or in a hybrid way with the support of online applications. This means that in the case of implementing solutions offered by Industry 4.0, they will experience a surge in efficiency growth, and the accomplished benefits from the application of modern technologies will exceed several times those large enterprises would count on. The situation of small and medium companies is extremely important, in context of adaptation of Industry 4.0 technologies. First, because in this way they have an opportunity to actively develop in the conditions of global cross-linked economies. Second, their competitiveness on international markets increases. Third, bearing in mind that the small and medium enterprise sector generates a significant part of GDP in any country, the future economic condition of the country will depend on the degree of SME digitization. Company size aside, it is necessary to notice that barriers related to the implementation of Industry 4.0 solutions are essentially similar for both groups, although there are also certain, sometimes important, barriers. Owing to the fact that their number is not small (see Figure 1.3), and the possibilities for their presentation scarce, the authors have decided to focus on those mentioned most often. One of the vital barriers hindering progress in the implementation of Industry 4.0 is the lack of courage on the part of managerial staff and business owners to perform deep changes. Indeed, the process of digital transformation requires vision, motivation and engagement from those who will perform it. Therefore, the concepts of Industry 4.0 cannot be implemented without Leadership 4.0, which is primarily related to (Lewin, 2017):

- enhanced flexibility of the decision-making process, in order to maximize the new opportunities in the organization, with simultaneous communication transparency,
- **proactive planning**[30] ahead of the course of events,
- fast identification and reaction by management to new competition appearing on the horizon,
- skillful utilization of talents of the people who can discover, use and maximize technological achievements,
- stimulation of the organization to take advantage of the opportunities offered by participation in a digital, global economy.

Bearing in mind the above, we thus see that lack of proper leadership when "passing" through the process of digital transformation in the organization is one of the reasons for managerial staff inactivity. Another barrier are the hazards related to cyber-security. Cooperation with other entities while implementing projects related to the Industry of the Future, which often involve sensitive data sharing, in fact creates concerns about the safety of the owned technological knowledge. The same fear accompanies owners for instance when they are remotely sharing any information assembled in data warehouses, concerning the whole production process of an organization. Therefore, bearing in mind the above, business owners must ask themselves the question whether their organization is prepared for

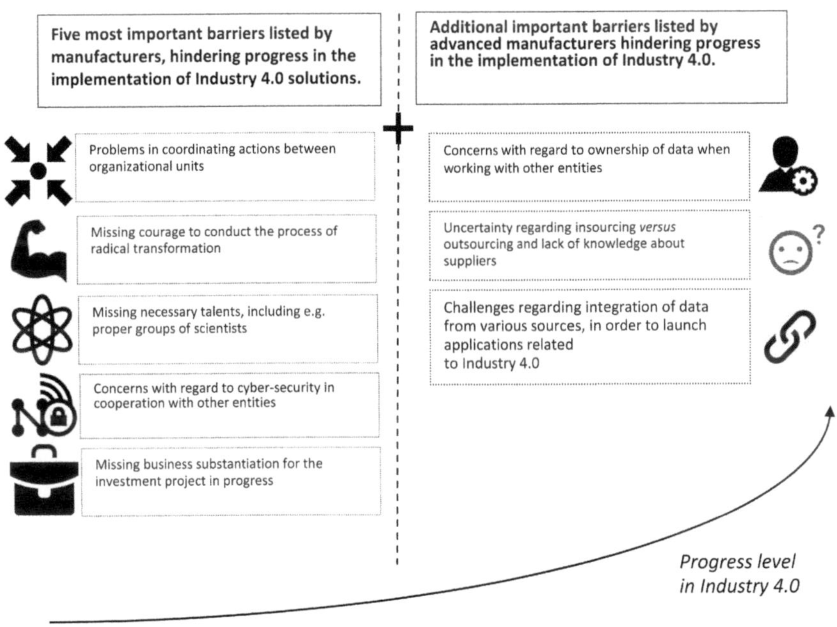

Figure 1.3 Barriers to Industry 4.0 implementation from the perspective of manufacturers. Source: Own study based on McKinsey and Company (2016).

data exposure to the external digital world, which is presently facing hazards, in the form of:

- attacks with the use of malicious software,
- attacks damaging collected data,
- attacks in order to extort confidential information by spoofing a trusted person or institution (phishing),[31]
- attacks causing denial of access to an application and thereby utilizing services and products offered online.

Thus, having such hazards in mind, preventive and security measures become of key importance to every organization, as at the right time they can quickly identify, categorize and eliminate a given hazard. Simultaneously, they can create appropriate defensive systems in case of further, similar attacks. An equally problematic barrier, from the point of view of the implementation of Industry 4.0 solutions in an organization, is one related to missing business justification for an investment project being implemented (see Figure 1.3). Finding arguments that would clearly justify an investment in Industry 4.0 is difficult for managers as this investment is not an ordinary one, because:

- it involves a transformation of the previous methods of organization management and personnel management,
- it often requires high financial outlays,
- it is difficult to plan funding necessary for its implementation,
- it is difficult to determine the time after which the investment returns or covers the implementation costs,
- it is not possible to compare it with other similar investments, as there are no good business cases in the given industry or sector,
- investment in modern technologies naturally bears higher risks,
- support, in particular legal and financial support, is missing both from the state and private investors.

Therefore, we see that investment projects related to Industry 4.0 are very complex and require a non-standard approach to implementation – the more so in that, from the economic point of view, we could ask what type of demand such investments are to satisfy and what is its estimated size. Certainly the answer to this question is neither easy nor unambiguous, and definitely requires a broader discussion. Special attention, when it comes to barriers hindering progress in the implementation of Industry 4.0, must be drawn to the challenges in integration of data from various sources (see Figure 1.3). In practice, a good example is a situation where consumers using various communication channels, equipment and screens leave a huge amount of data in systems which every company will then be forced to process, in order to stay on the market in the future. This requires appropriate systems that will quickly integrate data originating from different users, devices or from different digital and network channels. However, the optimization of business processes through more efficient exchange of information between various systems requires large financial outlays on data communications infrastructure and top class experts, who will be able to take advantage of the opportunities it offers e.g. in analyzing customer needs.

The barriers presented so far, which hinder the development of Industry 4.0 among enterprises, are only a small part of those that we can currently find in the professional literature or scientific literature covering this topic. Table 1.2 presents additional barriers that we may come across when exploring knowledge about Industry 4.0. Considering their essence and nature, they have been divided into three groups, including:

- barriers referring to legal and legislative problems,
- barriers referring to matters related to organization management,
- barriers referring to matters related to human resource management.

Owing to the fact that a description of all barriers would exceed the framework of this book, the authors have decided to describe only selected, previously undefined ones. In the case of legal barriers, important problems come in the form of matters concerning legal regulations both in the area of security and possibilities to implement new technologies. The geometric progress of technological progress makes any legislative changes unable to keep up. In consequence, there is an urgent need to remove legal barriers that today are not beneficial for the development of Industry 4.0 and, instead, create such legal frameworks in their place that will promote it. As an example, it is worth mentioning the delays present in the case of legal regulations related to unmanned aircraft, commonly referred to as drones. No relevant legal regulations presently prevent this technology from being fully used in such domains of the economy as logistics, finance or marketing. In the case of management, where the number of barriers seems to be the highest (see Table 1.2), a problem for many organizations is a tendency to create large **data silos** within their structures. Silos are nothing else but departments of marketing, sales, customer service, training, projects etc., that collect and analyze data only from their area and do not share with other departments. As a result, sales departments analyze only sales data, and marketing ones only marketing data. Finally, the lack of freeing-up of information leads to a gradual loss of competitive advantage by the organization, due to its inability to exchange data and thereby properly adapt to the changes taking place in its market environment. The last barrier discussed is concerned with a shortage of qualified specialists to work in Industry 4.0. In fact, the competence gap existing in this regard makes it necessary to take actions to change the present educational system, to ensure that it will better respond to the demands of the Industry of the Future in the area of human resources. However, awaiting these changes, employers will be forced to sustain often high costs of requalifying their employees. Moreover, the nature of the present labor market will also be transformed, as it will promote persons primarily having cognitive abilities and so-called meta-skills.[32]

Table 1.2 Industry 4.0 development barriers in organizations – a literature review

Barriers regarding	*Category*	*Authors/source*
Law	Missing standards.	(Schröder, 2017)
	No detailed regulations concerning technological innovation, in particular in the area of intellectual property, data protection and the scope of liability.	(Oesterreich & Teuteberg, 2016)
	No legal security for proprietary know-how.	(Siemens, 2017)
	No guidelines concerning work organization in the digital work environment.	(authors of the study)
Management	No initiative on the part of the management.	(Siemens, 2017)
	No digital strategy.	(Schröder, 2017)
	No well-designed IT department.	(Winberg & Ahrén, 2018)
	No suitable communication between the production department and IT.	(Siemens, 2017)
	No need to change the previous business model.	(Glass et al., 2018)
	No technological support inside the organization for the development of Industry 4.0.	(Yao et al., 2017)
	No data safety.	(Schröder, 2017)
	No transparency of information and production systems.	(Winberg & Ahrén, 2018)
	No partners for cooperation and project financing programs.	(Glass et al., 2018)
	No forecasts or evaluation of the effect of Industry 4.0 on the organization.	(Seseña Gaitán & López Martínez, 2017)
	Creating data silos.	(Yao et al., 2017); (Zheng et al., 2018)
	High risk of incorrect investments.	(Glass et al., 2018)
	Insufficient number of publications of business cases regarding successfully completed implementation projects in the domain of Industry 4.0.	(Siemens, 2017)
	High complexity of the topic.	(Glass et al., 2018)
	No planning of actions or implementation of solutions.	(Seseña Gaitán & López Martínez, 2017)
Human Resources	No qualified workforce (including: skills, knowledge, willingness to develop).	(Kagermann et al., 2013); (Glass et al., 2018)
	No visualization or understanding of dependencies in the man–machine interaction.	(Winberg & Ahrén, 2018)
	No strong leadership and change leaders.	(Fonseca, 2018)
	No experts.	(Siemens, 2017)
	No pressure for an increased degree of workforce flexibility.	(Glass et al., 2018)
	Negative demographic trends in highly developed countries of the world.	(authors of the study).

Source: Authors' own study.

To sum up the deliberations on the barriers hindering the development of Industry 4.0 in organizations, we should be aware that some of them can be eliminated or significantly limited, thanks to certain newly created frameworks of support conditions. The main focus here is on proposing such support instruments that would be conducive to the development and implementation of the technologies of the future in organizations, and which would be concerned primarily with a proper financial environment, access to highly qualified staff, utilization of access to high speed and broadband online links, or support from the state. In the case of the financial environment, a solution should be promoted that would assume that short-term research for Industry 4.0 would be mainly financed from enterprises' own funds, and long-term research would be supported by operating programs and grants on the part of the state, EU or other international organizations. Supplementary to this approach would be the possibility of financing innovative operations with support from external capital, offering credits, loans or debt securities on preferential terms for enterprises. An important element in financing the Industry of the Future, as is discussed currently, would be the popularization of the concept of **technological credits** that, apart from competitive interest, make it possible for the borrower to partially repay the credit in the case of completing the technological investment project.[33] While the creation of a proper financial environment for the development of Industry 4.0 is not a big problem, access to a qualified workforce definitely is. This is due to large shortages in key professions for the implementation of Industry 4.0 in, among others, information technology, electromechanics, automation, mechatronics and network technologies. Shortages in this area are caused by the closure of vocational schools[34] (especially in Central and Eastern European countries), which put great emphasis on teaching sciences, including mathematics, mechanics or automation, and the Western European trend of educating more persons in humanities (services) than in sciences (production). As a consequence, when still considering demographic changes, states will be forced to wait at least several years for the bridging of this gap. This creates excellent conditions for the development of education for schools and universities, which should match their offer of courses, majors and minors to the needs of the dynamically changing market. At the same time, they must put greater pressure than before on the education of engineers, computer scientists or technologists, and their courses should be more interdisciplinary and diverse. Apart from the support in the area of human resources, assistance is also necessary in access to fast, broadband Internet. This particularly applies to those enterprises that operate in rural areas or far from large metropolitan centers. Access to suitable fiber optic technology is essential from the point of view of Industry 4.0 development in general, and smart factories in particular. In this context, an important role can, and even should be played by the state, which, using its own budgetary funds, will enable entrepreneurs to access a wide-reaching, fast internet network. In addition, in the interests of the development of Industry 4.0, it should also fully finance those projects that in the near future will determine the country's new economic strength.

1.5 Industry 4.0 – challenges and opportunities for the organization and the global economy

Section 1.3 of this book has presented the economic potential "embedded" in the Fourth Industrial Revolution. Its recognition has been important as it indirectly generates a number of challenges that enterprises and nations will have to face on the way to the digital economy. Among the most important challenges on the microeconomic (enterprises') level, the following are distinguished in literature:

- removal of obstacles hindering the development of modern technologies,
- incentivizing managerial staff to change,
- need to redefine the present business model,
- data and communication security,
- access to fast, broadband internet,
- creation of databases along with necessary methods for their analysis,
- maintenance of the integrity of manufacturing processes,
- construction of reliable machine–machine communication,
- protection of specialist technological and industrial knowledge against competition,
- access to qualified workforce,
- access to knowledge related to Industry 4.0.

When it comes to the macroeconomic (nation) level, the following are mainly regarded as the most important challenges:

- the need to consider the concepts of Industry 4.0 in international legal regulations,
- particularization of legal regulations concerning Industry 4.0 in the areas of ethics, security and intellectual property,
- preparation of government strategies for the development of Industry 4.0 at the level of individual countries,
- creation of operating programs financing the development of Industry 4.0 projects,
- filling the gaps existing in the data communications infrastructure (system gaps),
- removal of the employee gap related to the large shortage of experts on the global labor market,
- change of the present model of education at the level of high schools and universities,
- development of a scenario considering possible social exclusion and civilization threats related to the development of Industry 4.0.

Although for most countries the challenges related to the development of the Industry of the Future are the same, as suggested by Petrillo et al. (2018), they may slightly differ from each other, especially when divided into developed and developing countries. In their opinion (Petrillo et al., 2018) for a developed country, the implementation of solutions in the domain of Industry 4.0 additionally involves:

- the need to perform frequent experiments and continuously improve, to ensure that knowledge and experience obtained in this way could serve other companies in strengthening their operations,
- the need to "free" data so that information could be sent faster and in large quantities,
- transformation of the workforce, including the integration of system operators with new skills, which allow digital work management using CPS systems.

On the other hand, challenges faced by developing states center on:

- building a holistic training system to allow equipment operators to acquire specific skills in the area of digital manufacturing and management,
- increasing the scale of implementation of the leading technologies from Industry 4.0,
- identifying sources of external funding for the development of the digital economy.

In the context of the above, it should be noticed that in the case of the developing countries, many of the challenges that are placed before them, in the context of the Fourth Industrial Revolution, have not yet been taken up. However, lively discussions about the Industry of the Future are underway in many areas, and the related conceptual works are often at the initial stage of development. Meanwhile, in developed countries, which are considered leaders in the implementation of Industry 4.0 technologies (see Table 1.3), some of the listed challenges either have already been fully addressed, or their implementation is very advanced. As an example, it is worth mentioning the challenge related to the exchange of knowledge and experience of various entities regarding Industry 4.0, for this information to serve other companies in strengthening their operations in this area; in many countries this task has already been accomplished, the effect of which is presence of the Industry 4.0 Platforms, which allow for coordination of private and public activities in context of the tasks and projects related to Industry 4.0. Currently, they operate in many EU and other countries, including Germany (*Plattform Industrie 4.0*), Austria (*Verein Industrie 4.0 Österreich – die Plattform für intelligente Produktion*), Switzerland (*Initiative "Industrie 2025"*), France (*Alliance Industrie du Futur*), Spain (*Industria Conectada 4.0*), Italy (*Piano Industria 4.0*), Poland (*Platforma Przemysłu Przyszłości*), Czech Republic (*Národní Centrum Průmyslu 4.0*, NCP 4.0), Finland (*Reboot IoT Factory*) or China (*中国制造2025_中国政府网*). However, this example also makes us aware of the increasing disparities between developed and developing countries in the context of their readiness for the implementation of Industry 4.0 technologies. In practice, this means further growth of the development gap and decreasing competitiveness

Table 1.3 Leading nations of the Fourth Industrial Revolution

No.	*Country*	*Industry 4.0 – description of readiness*
1.	Canada	Already for several years now, Canada has been perceived as the world center of innovative technologies. Most frequently, they are related to artificial intelligence, scattered registers or incremental manufacturing. In addition, next to Germany and Japan, Canada is best adapted to the upcoming wave of changes in the context of the development of digital economies. Importantly, the government of Canada has impressive possibilities of financing innovative business projects for the development of Industry 4.0.
2.	Japan	Japan is one of the leading countries in the world in terms of production volume. However, currently, it faces many social challenges related e.g. to the ageing of the society. However, this country's authorities are certain that they will overcome these problems with the help of Industry 4.0. Therefore, the "Society 5.0" idea has already been popularized in the country for some time now with the intention of solving social problems using Industry 4.0 technologies. Japan also ranks high among the most robotized countries worldwide.
3.	Germany	Germany is the first country in Europe and one of the world leaders in terms of industrial production volume. Since 2016 the government in Berlin has had an updated *Hightech* development strategy for Germany. Companies in Germany are encouraged by various support programs to implement innovative technologies from the area of artificial intelligence into their products and services. Cooperation of the business world with education as well as assistance for innovative startups, along with a dialogue economy–politics–social organizations–business, are achieved by an institution referred to as "*Platform Industrie 4.0*". Germany is also determined in pursuing an implementation program for state-of-the-art technologies in the domain of Industry 4.0 to the six major economy sectors: the machine, electrotechnical, automotive, chemical industries as well as agriculture and the data communication industry.
4.	Australia	Australia is one of the leading countries in the world in terms of production process automation. Recently, leaders of the largest industrial groups in this country have made a decision to increase incentives for companies interested in the automation and digitization of their manufacturing. In addition, in 2017 a workgroup formed by the Prime Minister of Australia signed a cooperation agreement with German company Platform Industrie 4.0. The purpose of this initiative is mutual collaboration and exchange of experience for the development of Industry 4.0 technologies in both these countries. Australia was one of five countries to conclude such a cooperation agreement with Germany.
5.	Austria	Austria is characterized by a very high degree of industrialization, therefore Industry 4.0 is a necessary element of the further development of this country's industrial processes. Apart from Germany, Austria has the largest potential in the industry for the implementation of smart manufacturing processes and automation. In 2014 a platform was created in this country modelled after Germany's (*Industrie 4.0 Österreich*) for the exchange of ideas and experience of various circles and parties on the technologies and concepts of Industry 4.0.

(*Continued*)

Table 1.3 (Continued)

No.	*Country*	*Industry 4.0 – description of readiness*
6.	Switzerland	The Swiss industry is commonly recognized as one of the best environments for effective implementation of Industry 4.0 concepts. Currently, Switzerland actively part in the "Industry 2025" initiative, the aim of which is to develop the Industry 4.0 problem areas in Switzerland and promote sustainable digital transformation of the Swiss industry.

Source: Authors' own study.

between these country groups, which can give rise to notable anxiety. Hence, at this point we should ask whether the Fourth Industrial Revolution will reduce, or rather will it increase the economic distance that divides the developed from the developing countries.

Owing to the fact that the answer to this question is ambiguous and has many aspects, the authors have decided to leave it for individual consideration by the readers.

The presented challenges that are faced by business owners, managerial staff, state authorities or the employees themselves in building the digital economy are characterized by the fact that, apart from the required effort everyone has to offer to address them, they also create certain opportunities. In the case of Industry 4.0 they are related to (UNIDO, 2017):

- improvement in enterprises' financial performance, primarily due to revenue growth as a result of lower transaction and transport costs,
- increased efficiency and quality of the products and services offered,
- transition to mass customization with an increased participation by the small and medium enterprises sector,
- development of subsequent innovations in the area of applications, resulting in a greater impact on economic growth,
- manufacturing that is energy-efficient and environmentally friendly,
- more effective use of human, property, natural resources,
- increased food safety for different regions of the world,
- increased personal security,
- improved state of health and safety of employees,
- changes in education and training systems,
- easier access to innovative technologies (see Figure 1.4),
- changes in work organization, transition from office-based work to teleworking,
- solving demographic problems.

Opportunities in the development of the Fourth Industrial Revolution other than those indicated by the United Nations Industrial Development Organization (UNIDO) experts are shown by e.g. Xu et al. (2018) and primarily include:

- lower barriers between inventors and markets,
- greater scope for action by artificial intelligence (AI),
- integration of diverse techniques and sectors (technological fusion[35]),
- improvement in the quality of life (robotization of life),
- growing integrity of life (the Internet).

All of the above opportunities created by the Industry of the Future are assessed by Xu et al. (2018). First, with reference to the existing inventor–market barriers, the authors anticipate that the development of modern technologies (see Figure 1.4) may lead to their significant limitation. To confirm their words, they use

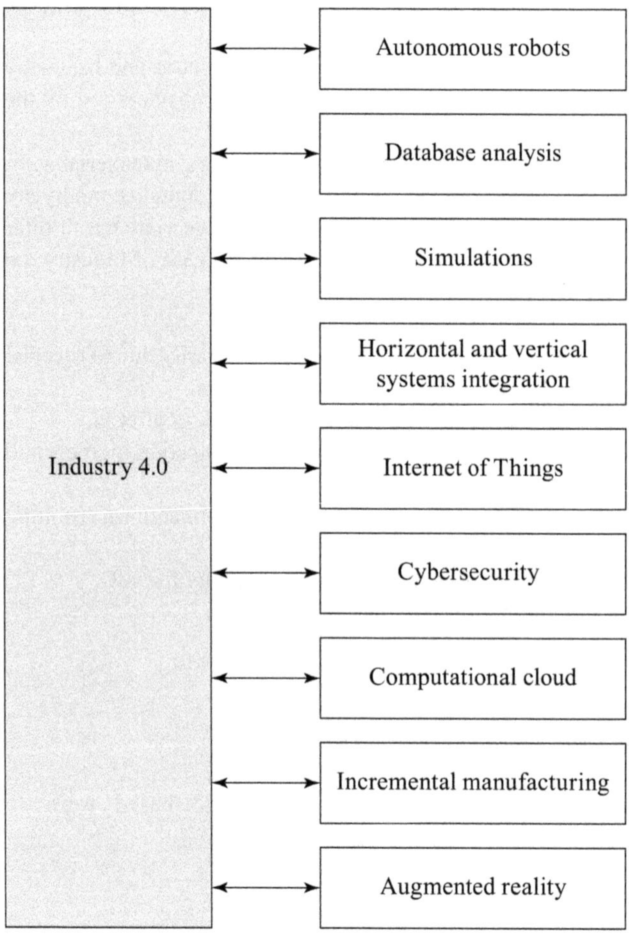

Figure 1.4 Industry 4.0 – technologies of the future. Source: The Boston Consulting Group (2015).

the example of 3D printing, which already offers entrepreneurs the possibility to introduce a new product to the market more quickly, due to the elimination of limitations existing before in this area, with regard to time or costs of creating prototypes. Second, as compared to artificial intelligence and its utilization prospects, the authors claim that artificial systems will create new opportunities for economic growth for many countries. In fact, the automation of production and business processes progressing at a geometric pace already allows companies to save billions of dollars and create new jobs. While autonomous cars will be able to replace drivers to a certain extent e.g. from Uber, autonomous trucks will radically transform the courier shipments market, resulting in a significant reduction in jobs for truck drivers. Third, concepts regarding the development of technological fusions have huge potential because, as already signaled earlier, they blur the lines between the physical, digital and biological spheres (Dombrowski & Wagner, 2014). This combination of technologies goes far beyond the previous boundaries for the meanings of the words "integration", "consolidation" or "unification". Technological fusion is something more than a mutually supplementing technology, because it creates new product markets and new opportunities for every innovator. It allows new products and services to be created, often from elements that were previously separate. Fourth, unprecedented opportunities will be related to the progressing robotization of life. Technical robots will not only cook, or create music for us, but will drive our cars, or replace surgeons in the operating theater. With their omnipresence, the quality of our lives will be improved, either at home, at work, or in other areas. In the opinion of Xu et al. (2018), robots will improve the quality of existing workplaces and give people more time to focus on what is of interest to them and what they like doing. And fifth, it is expected that, with the Internet of Things, humanity will be able to take advantage of a number of opportunities from the existence of advanced communication between devices, systems or services, which will go beyond the present machine–machine communication paradigm and will also encompass various protocols, domains and applications (Xu et al., 2018).

To sum up this chapter on the challenges and opportunities that are involved in the development of the Fourth Industrial Revolution, it must be concluded that in most cases they will be determined by the individual commitment to this concept by both enterprises and states. Still, the leading role in this process should be taken by enterprises, for which an opportunity to instantly participate in the development of the global digital economy should be treated as a "preemptive strike", ahead of actions by competitors. On the other hand, the role of the state must, simultaneously, concentrate on the construction of the whole organizational–legal–financial structure around Industry 4.0, the quality of which will ultimately determine the pace and the scale of absorption of innovative technologies by domestic enterprises. Therefore, the platforms related to the Industry of the Future already being developed in many countries, as the place for exchanging ideas and knowledge but also for meetings of inventors with manufacturers or manufacturers with consumers, should be considered a step in the right direction. In addition, when considering the pace of development of Industry 4.0, both developing and developed countries should be particularly alert here. The challenge, from the global point of view, is to avoid a situation in which dynamic growth in technological innovation of enterprises in developed countries results in a significant enlargement of the development gap (including financial and intellectual) with developing countries. In fact, this dichotomy would enhance the risk of losing a substantial portion of the benefits attributed to the idea of Industry 4.0. Therefore, a question arises whether an authority should not be created at the global level, or a working team appointed, under the auspices of the World Bank or UN for example, to coordinate and supervise activities related to the developmental dynamics of the Fourth Industrial Revolution in particular regions of the world. It seems that only this solution would offer a guarantee of permanent and sustainable development of this concept at the global level.

Notes

1 Thomas Newcomen (1664–1729) – a British mechanic, commonly known as the inventor of the piston steam machine. Newcomen built the steam engine with the help of J. Calley in a coal mine, Coneygree, near Dudley Castle in the Midlands. According to preserved archive data, the machine was 17 meters high and operated continuously completing 12 working cycles per minute, with over 5 horsepower. It commonly served to evaporate underground water from flooded mines.

2 James Neilson (1792–1865) – a British metallurgist and inventor, who in 1828 patented the process of smelting metals with the use of hot air explosion (regenerative heating).

3 George Stephenson (1871–1848) – a British engineer and inventor, commonly regarded as the "father of British steam railway". Designed by Stephenson as early as in 1814, the first steam locomotive, named "Blücher", was able to pull 30 tons of coal on tracks at the speed of 6 km/h. The next steam locomotive named "Locomotion", built in 1825, was already able to pull 80 tons of coal and achieve a speed high as 39 km/h.

4 For more information, see: Friedmann (1936).

5 The telegraph was invented by Samuel Morse in the first half of the 19th century. On 24 May 1844, the alphabet created by Morse sent, from Washington to Baltimore, the first message in history by the use of an electric telegraph. In addition, Morse is also considered as the inventor of the marble cutting machine, which enables the creation of three-dimensional shapes.

6 Alexander Bell is commonly regarded as the inventor of telephone, as he was the first to patent his invention. However, it was Antonio Meucci who equipped the unit with voice communication and made it become in fact the prototype of the telephone. Unlike Bell, Meucci did not have sufficient funds to pay for the patent resulting in all credit related to telephone invention being taken by Bell. In this context, discussions and disputes are held to this day as to who should actually be regarded as the inventor of the telephone.

7 Brothers Orville Wright and Wilbur Wright are considered the designers of the first airplane. On 14 December 1903 Wilbur Wright made the first fully controlled, airplane flight over a distance of 279 meters.

8 Programmable Logic Controller, PLC.

9 It is worth mentioning here that in the opinion of some representatives of the European Union, from 2020, almost a third of the electric energy used in the Member States came from renewable energy sources.

10 Digital ecosystems are networks (platforms) of connected services allowing users to satisfy various needs with their held competences. Thus, digital ecosystems help associate customer needs with the offer of independent suppliers on the basis of the platform owner's strong brand.

11 See Note 10.

12 China, having large financial resources at present, for several years has been implementing the policy of buying out high-tech companies both in Europe and United States. As an example, it is worth mentioning the largest private Chinese automotive corporation Geely, which as early as in 2010 bought the rights to the production of Swedish Volvo vehicles, for USD 1.8 billion from Ford Motor Company. In 2016, to the surprise of this vehicle brand's fans, Geely corporation representatives announced that from then on the latest version of the S90 would be produced only in China and distributed worldwide from there. What is more, using Volvo technologies, by 2018 the corporation started building cars for the needs of its own proprietary brand Lynk & Co., with sales worldwide, as the cheaper alternative to Volvo vehicles. At present, Geely corporation is perceived by market experts as the fastest developing car manufacturer in the world.

13 For more information, see: www.bmbf.de/en/index.html.

14 The concept of Industry 4.0 can most concisely be defined as a combination and interaction of the physical world with the virtual one.

15 According to the web portal dreamgrow.com the number of active Facebook users was estimated at more than 2.2 billion persons monthly in 2018.

16 In 2015 US analytical and research company Gartner, based in Stamford, Conn., considered the **Internet of Everything** as one of the most important trends worldwide.

17 This is a higher level of compatibility.

18 Generally, we can say that meta-skills are certain abilities allowing a person to effectively function in the rapidly changing reality or environment.

19 Roland Berger Strategy Consultants was established in 1967 and is one of the leading consulting companies worldwide. The company runs operations in more than 36 countries worldwide and provides services in consulting and strategic management for large international concerns.

20 Excessive deficit procedure (EDP) is applied on an EU member state if this state's budget deficit permanently exceeds 3 percent of the GDP. It should be mentioned that in 2009, the excessive deficit procedure covered as many as 20 among 28 EU member states.

21 This applies to digital support of the power industry in areas related to: network reliability, intelligent reaction to demand, integration of renewable energy sources, or implementation of a smart charging method for eclectic vehicles.

22 Critical infrastructures are actual and cybernetic facilities, devices or installed systems necessary to ensure the minimum functioning of the economy and the state itself. Critical infrastructure usually consist of the following: power supply systems, energy resources and fuels, communication systems, data communication networks, financial systems, water and food supply systems, health protection systems and general living protection systems, transport systems, etc.

23 According to the definition proposed by European Telecommunications Standards Institute 2015 (standard: ETSI TR 103 290 v1.1.1, 2015-04) a city may be considered smart, if investment in the human and social capital as well as traditional transport and modern communication infrastructure are the driving force in sustainable economic development and high quality of life, with rational management of natural resources by civil society.

24 At present, China is considered the country with the highest number of CCTV cameras worldwide: in 2017 it operated more than 170 million of them. Another 400 million were installed by the end of 2020.

25 After turning 16 each China citizen is obliged to present to the respective state authorities his or her identification document, as part of building the Chinese security supervision network Skynet.
26 For instance, within a smart storm water management system, which makes water consumption more efficient and profitable.
27 Intelligence management is the term mainly applied with regard to all actions, processes or decisions in the Industry 4.0 environment, consisting of a wide range of highly advanced technologies and concepts, the application of which to the resources held, including digital technologies, will ensure that the organization will achieve the intended goals.
28 The fundamental reason why Kodak ignored the digital revolution in the photography market referred to the profit margin: traditional photography, which Kodak benefited from in billions of dollars, generated a profit margin of 60%, while the digital one only 15%.
29 In the 20th century in the United States the Kodak Company engineers were granted almost 20 000 patents.
30 The opposite to proactive planning, focused on taking the initiative and searching for new solutions, is reactive planning mostly focused on fulfilling someone else's requests and orders as well as solving others' and not one's own problems.
31 According to data published on 12 March 2019 on their website by the Kaspersky company, one of the largest cyber-security businesses worldwide, in 2018 the number of phishing attacks in the world was estimated at 500 million, which implies in practice that it increased more than twice compared to 2017.
32 See Note 18.
33 Such an approach in financing innovative activities is defined as a technological bonus.
34 The liquidation of professional schools in Central and Eastern Europe was mainly caused by the fact that until the end of the 1990s those schools were considered as places "offering education" to the unemployed. This was important because the vast majority of the countries in the region were fighting a high unemployment rate at that time, which in fact had been "inherited" after the communist times.
35 The concept of technological fusion is to be understood as a combination and transformation of a series of various technologies that result in new products and markets being created. Technological fusions are a result of mutual expenses, research and development of companies originating from various industries and characterized by different competences.

References

Anderl, R. (2014). Industrie 4.0: Advanced engineering of smart products and smart production. In 19° Seminário Internacional de Alta Tecnologia – Inovações Tecnológicas no Desenvolvimento do Produto, Piracicaba, Brasil.

Blanche, M., Rinn, T., Von Thaden, G., & De Thieulloy, G. (2014). *Industry 4.0. The New Industrial Revolution: How Europe Will Succeed.* Munich: Roland Berger Strategy Consultants GMBH.

Deloitte, A. G. (2015). *Industry 4.0. Challenges and Solutions for the Digital Transformation and Use of Exponential Technologies.* Zurich: The Creative Studio at Deloitte.

Dombrowski, U., & Wagner T. (2014). Mental strain as field of action in the 4th industrial revolution. *Procedia CIRP*, *17*, pp. 100–105.

Espinasse, F., & Donnachie, I. Neilson, James Beaumont (1792–1865). Engineer and inventor of the hot blast in iron manufacture. Oxford Dictionary of National Biography.

Retrieved 23 July 2021 from: https://www.oxforddnb.com/view/10.1093/ref:odnb/9780198614128.001.0001/odnb-9780198614128-e-19866.

European Commission. (2016). *Research Workshop on Digitising the Agri-food Sector: A Research Agenda for Horizon 2020*. Brussels: Directorate General for Agriculture and Rural Development. Downloaded from: https://ec.europa.eu/newsroom/horizon2020/document.cfm?doc_id=40233.

Flex International Ltd. (2019). *How Industry 4.0 Will Virtually Erase Downtime and Save You Money*. Downloaded 1 August 2019 from: https://flex.com/insights/live-smarter-blog/how industry-40-will-virtually-erase-downtime-and-save-you-money.

Fonseca, L. M. (2018). Industry 4.0 and the digital society: Concepts, dimensions and envisioned benefits. In Proceedings of the International Conference on Business Excellence, Vol. 12, pp. 386–395. DOI: 10.2478/picbe-2018-0034.

Friedmann, G. (1936). *La Crise du progrès: esquisse d'histoire des idées, 1895–1935*. Paris: Gallimard.

Glass, R., Meissner, A., Gebauer, Ch., Sturmer, S., & Metternich, J. (2018). Identifying the barriers to Industrie 4.0. In 51st CIRP Conference on Manufacturing Systems, Stockholm, Sweden.

Hermann, M., Pentek, T., & Otto, B. (2016). Design principles for Industrie 4.0 scenarios. In 49th Hawaii International Conference on System Sciences, IEEE, Koloa, HI, USA.

Kagermann, H., Wahlster, W., & Helbig, J. (2013). *Recommendations for Implementing the Strategic Initiative Industrie 4.0*. Linda Treugut, M.A. and acatech - Frankfurt: National Academy of Science and Engineering.

Kirby, M. Stephenson, George (1781–1848). colliery and railway engineer. Oxford Dictionary of National Biography. Retrieved 23 July 2021 from: https://www.oxforddnb.com/view/10.1093/ref:odnb/9780198614128.001.0001/odnb-9780198614128-e-26397.

Kuznets, S. (1965). *Economic Growth and Structure*. New York: W.W. Nortonan.

Lewin, N. (2017). *All Change for Industry 4.0*. Denkendorf: Festo Training & Consulting.

Liffler, M., & Tschiesner, A. (2013). *The Internet ofThings and the Future of Manufacturing*. Stuttgart, Munich: McKinsey & Company.

Maslarić, M., Nikoličić, S., & Mirčetić, D. (2016). Logistics response to the industry 4.0: The physical internet. *Open Eng.*, *6*, pp. 511–517. DOI: 10.1515/eng-2016-0073.

McKinsey & Company. (2016). *Industry 4.0 after the Initial Hype. Where Manufacturers are Finding Value and How They Can Best Capture It*. Berlin: McKinsey Digital.

Mokyr, J., & Strotz, H. R. (2000). *The Second Industrial Revolution, 1870–1914*. Downloaded 1 June 2019 from: https://www.semanticscholar.org/paper.

Oesterreich, T. D., & Teuteberg, F. (2016). Understanding the implications of digitisation and automation in the context of Industry 4.0: A triangulation approach and elements of a research agenda for the construction industry. *Computers in Industry*, *83*, pp. 121–139.

Petrillo, A., De Felice, F., Cioffi, R., & Zomparelli, F. (2018). Fourth industrial revolution: Current practices, challenges, and opportunities. *IntechOpen*, p. 10. DOI: 10.5772/intechopen.72304.

Pottin, F., & Dietz, T. (2018). Automation goes 4.0: The"SMART"AACfactory. *Ce/papers, 2018*, pp. 25–28. DOI: org/10.1002/cepa.898.

PwC. (2016). *Industry 4.0: Building the Digital Enterprise*. Munich, Gemany: PwC.

Rajkumar, R., Lee, I., Sha, L., & Stankovic, J. (2010) Cyber-physical systems: The next computing revolution. In Design Automation Conference 2010, Anaheim, CA.

Rifkin, J. (2012). The third industrial revolution: How the internet, green electricity, and 3-D printing are ushering in a sustainable era of distributed capitalism. *World Financ. Rev., 2012*, pp. 8–12.

Rüßmann, M., Lorenz, M., Gerbert, P., Waldner, M., Engel, P., Harnisch, M., Justus, J. (2015). *Industry 4.0: The Future of Productivity and Growth in Manufacturing Industries*. Boston: Boston Consulting Group.

Schröder, Ch. (2017). *The Challenges of Industry 4.0 for Small and Medium-sized Enterprises*. Bonn: Friedrich-Ebert-Stiftung, Division for Economic and Social Policy.

Schwab, K. (2016). *The Fourth Industrial Revolution*. Cologny/Geneva: Penguin Books Ltd.

Seseña Gaitán, D., & López Martínez, Í. (2017). Five errors in the implementation of Industry 4.0. How to be ready for the digitalization roll-out. Downloaded 1 September 2019 from: https://www.minsait.com/sites/default/files/newsroom_documents/five_errors_in_the_implementation_of_industry_4.pdf.

Siemens. (2017). Od industry 4.0 do smart factory. Downloaded 1 August 2019 from: https://www.siemens.pl/industry-40.

Smit, J., Kreutzer, S., Moeller, C., & Carlberg, M. (2016). *Industry 4.0* (Report No. IP/A/ITRE/2015-02). Brussels: European Parliament, Directorate-General for Internal Policies.

United Nations Industrial Development Organization (UNIDO). (2017). Industry 4.0: The opportunities behind the challenge. In General Conference, Partnering for Impact: Achieving the Sustainable Development Goals, Department of Trade, Investment and Innovation, Vienna International Centre, Vienna, Austria. United Nations Industrial Development Organization (UNIDO).

Winberg, E., & Ahrén, J. (2018). *Industry 4.0 from a Technology Adoption Perspective*. Stockholm: The Royal Institute of Technology.

Wong, S., Wan, J., Li, D., & Zhang, C. (2016). Implementing smart factory of industry 4.0: An outlook. *Int. J. Distrib. Sens. Netwo.*, *12*(1), p. 2. DOI: org/10.1155/2016/3159805.

Xu, M., David, J. M., & Hi Kim, S. (2018). The fourth industrial revolution: Opportunities and challenges. *Int. J. Financ. Res.*, *12*, pp. 90–94. DOI: 10.5430/ijfr.v9n2p90.

Yao, X. et al. (2017). Smart manufacturing based on cyber-physical systems and beyond. *J. Intell. Manuf.* (Peer-reviewed), 13 December, *30*, p. 13.

Zheng, P., et al. (2018). Smart manufacturing systems for Industry 4.0: Conceptual framework, scenarios, and future perspectives. *Front. Mech. Eng.* (Peer-reviewed), 27 September, *13*(2), pp. 137–150.

2 Artificial intelligence (AI) – a new technology in the postmodern era

2.1 Artificial intelligence – an explanation-based perspective

It is worth noting that Artificial Intelligence (AI) is a scientific discipline and, therefore, a research activity focused on searching for and systematizing information and possibilities to apply it in practice. Its origins date back to the early 1950s, when scientists noticed that if a computer can be programmed to solve simple mathematical tasks, other machines can equally well, with sufficient information, demonstrate broader, human-like intelligence (Bowser et al., 2017). The term **artificial intelligence** was used for the first time in 1955 by outstanding mathematician and computer scientist John McCarthy.[1] A year later, at the famous conference in Dartmouth, which formally was a summer research project on artificial intelligence (AI), McCarthy introduced the concept of artificial intelligence into circulation worldwide. After that, a significant period of work and research on AI started, which has continued until the present day. Its first stage occurred during the 1950s. Initially, achievements related to this area were concerned first of all with **heuristic search** and **machine learning**. Heuristic search[2] methods that were developed allowed above all allowed the creation of the initial, new algorithms to solve defined problems or limit high costs related to their computational complexity. In the case of machine learning, the foundations were laid for its present architecture, primarily related to deep learning. However, achievements in these areas were yet to become the foundation for the construction of solutions in image recognition technology, natural language processing or robotics. The 1960s were characterized by the development of professional research centers the operations of which were focused around works on AI. The first of these were established at the Massachusetts Institute of Technology (MIT) in Cambridge, at the Carnegie Mellon University (CMU) in Pittsburgh and at Stanford University. However, due to the pressure exerted at the time by investors and the private sector on commercialization of AI solutions, the US government quickly decided to commence funding of research on AI development with participation and under the auspices of the governmental Defense Advanced Research Projects Agency (DARPA). The primary goal was to accelerate the application of AI theory in practice. Such an approach was perceived as being of key importance not so much from the point of view of the economic growth of the United

DOI: 10.4324/9781003184027-2

States as its national defense and security. In fact, the first technological solutions in AI area were to serve and be used above all by the American military. In the 1970s a valuable contribution to the development of research on AI was made by American mathematician Richard Bellman.[3] As the creator of **dynamic programming** he developed a technique of designing algorithms, which has been broadly applied in solving optimization problems. As a result, his ideas were used to solve computer decision-making-related dilemmas (Bellman, 1978). Contrary to the previous decades, the beginning of the 1980s marked a slowdown in the development of AI-related concepts. The disappointment within the scientific community in this regard was large enough for this period to be referred to in the literature as "the winter period in artificial intelligence" (Bowser et al., 2017). The main barrier to AI development at that time was the small size of computers and inadequate computational power when working on complex AI algorithms and models. In consequence, the pace of innovative solutions from the domain of algorithmics,[4] related, for example, to neural networks could not be regarded as satisfactory during that era. However, a turnaround occurred in the 1990s and the work on AI intensified again, thanks to improvements in the production of complex integrated circuits and a gradual growth in the computational power, connected with the dynamic development of software, which made possible the first, efficient and widely available algorithms using artificial intelligence-based solutions. Moreover, the rapid growth and gradual popularization in daily life of mini-computers and computer systems paved the way for new technological solutions regarding artificial visual perception, artificial awareness, advanced control techniques or speech signal processing. A consequence of the achievements in AI at the end of the 20th century was the popularization, at the onset of the 21st century, of production process automation as well as a surge in robotics and cybernetics, allowing AI to function in various domains of life. It is clear that its growing omnipresence could not have been possible without the dynamic development of the Internet, cellular telephony, or other mobile technologies later in the new millennium. The popularity of AI is also clearly noticeable in the scientific field, with an almost tenfold increase in the number of publications on the topic, compared to those published in 2000. In recent years, most articles concerning this topic have been published in China, the United States and Europe. Since 2010 we can also observe a trend related to the largest technology companies worldwide, including Microsoft, Google, Apple, Amazon, Alphabet, Alibaba, Netflix or Tencent, taking over technological startups in order to build their own knowledge databases in the area of artificial intelligence.[5] Most frequently "absorbed" have been the companies possessing within their competencies practical solutions related to speech, sound, image processing as well as business services. Scientific progress, commercialization of research and the social reactions we can observe in the last few years in the field of AI in many countries have also placed the problem at the core of political interest. As a consequence, national strategies for research and development of artificial intelligence are being established at the governmental level. In addition, the implications, both tangible and intangible, that AI may cause are being discussed in areas related to safety, labor markets, socio-economic development, legal regulations, morality or ethics. Therefore, as AI is becoming a dominant subject in the global discussions about politics and economy, it is more and more important to find answers to various questions such as: how the related benefits and threats will develop in the future, will AI help to solve the humanity's problems such as hunger, lifestyle diseases and epidemics, global warming, homelessness or terrorism, and will AI outgrow human intelligence?

With knowledge about the circumstances in which the term "artificial intelligence" was coined and how this scientific discipline has developed over the last six decades, it is now time to take a closer look at how it is defined in the literature. As in the case of many other definitions, this concept can also "boast" of a wealth of interpretations in science; however, the two main perspectives can be classified as a broad and a narrow one. **Artificial intelligence** in the narrow perspective (narrow AI) means the ability of machines and systems to collect and use knowledge and demonstrate intelligent behaviors. In practice, they are most frequently related to several cognitive tasks and relate mostly to detection, spoken language processing, reasoning, learning and decision-making. In addition, they can control and move various types of objects. At the same time, intelligent systems utilize a combination of connections between large data collections, computational clouds, machine–machine communication and IoT for work and science (OECD, 2016; UNCTAD, 2017). A different example, concise in comparison to the previous one, of the narrow perspective on the AI definition is proposed by Manyika and Bughin (2018), who believe that artificial intelligence involves solving specific problems, for example related to natural language processing, with the use of machine learning techniques. Here it is necessary to add that artificial intelligence works by combining large amounts of both input and output data with fast iterative processing and intelligent algorithms. As a result, a program learns autonomously by identifying certain data patterns (Latentview, 2018). In the broad perspective (general AI) artificial intelligence is often defined as a specific type of system that can rationally solve multi-dimensional problems or take actions to accomplish earlier adopted goals. An important supplement to this definition is the idea proposed by Bellman (1978), which draws attention to the fact that all the actions associated with artificial intelligence take place both in an automated manner and while utilizing human thinking processes mostly related to decision-making, problem-solving or learning. An interesting definition of this notion was also proposed by its creator himself, John McCarthy (see note 1 in this chapter), who regarded artificial intelligence as the science and the engineering of creating smart machines. His proposal seems to correspond well with the contemporary one, which in an almost trivial way concludes that artificial intelligence is simply the science of doing smart things. Although in the subject literature the concept of artificial intelligence has many interpretations, both more general and narrower ones, so far it has not been possible to develop one, commonly adopted definition that could serve as a certain type of paradigm in the discussions on the nature of AI. However, for the purposes of this publication we will define artificial intelligence as "a collection of revolutionary technologies that, using smart machines and equipment, allow human abilities to be augmented in the triangle data–environment–man, mostly thanks to action, interaction, detection and the learning process". In the context of the above, it should be noted that the understanding of what artificial intelligence is in the narrow and broad perspectives is necessary, but insufficient to capture its essence and nature. Therefore, additionally, it is necessary to acquire knowledge about weak and strong artificial intelligence and superintelligence. In the scientific world it is assumed that in general there are two types of artificial intelligence, namely weak[6] and strong.[7] The former one, weak AI, means that by simulation a computer only becomes similar to human intelligence. As a result, it is a tool used e.g. for the examination of cognitive processes. In the practice of everyday life it comes down to the production of useful machines and equipment the design of which allows better and faster performance of work, as compared to the human. This also applies to any tasks that on a daily basis exceed both our mental and physical abilities. Experts from Accenture (2018) agree that weak artificial intelligence is in fact a description of simulated thinking.[8] In consequence, a system that seems to behave intelligently in fact has no awareness of what is going on. As an example, they point to chatbot (linguabot), a computer software that runs a conversation with us with the use of natural language, still having no awareness of who it is and why it is talking with us. However, it makes an impression of being smart enough for the interlocutor to be convinced that he or she is talking with a living person. The second type of artificial intelligence, strong AI, is characterized by the fact that the processes in the computer are of an intellectual and self-learning nature; therefore, they have the attributes typical of the human mind. Consequently, computers, using relevant software, can "comprehend" what is going on and are able to optimize their own behavior on the basis of previous actions and experiences. All this is possible primarily due to the automatic connection of particular computer units, first with a network, and then with other machines operating as part of the AI. It is also necessary to know that in the philosophy of artificial intelligence there is no fundamental difference between software being artificial intelligence resembling the human brain's operation and human activities, including those related to understanding, awareness or learning. Contrary to weak artificial intelligence, strong AI describes real and not simulated thinking (Accenture, 2018). It is based on smart behavior and understanding, as in the case of humans – we can compare this to a conversation between two people who, in all probability, know well who they are, what they are doing, where and why. Currently, games are one of the most popular places where strong artificial intelligence is used. Although strong artificial intelligence is a key (strategic) part of the AI-related revolution, weak artificial intelligence is more widespread, however, scientists agree that the former is a genuine representation of human intelligence in machines. A confirmation of those words is that, with strong artificial intelligence, machines as well as other devices can independently think and perform actions that follow humans. In the case of weak artificial intelligence, unfortunately, machines do not have such possibilities, which means that tasks performed by them largely require human intervention. Unlike weak AI, strong AI also features a complex algorithm that affects its "independence", while all the actions in weak artificial intelligence systems are initially programmed by humans. In practice, this means that machines driven by strong artificial intelligence can process and make "their own" decisions while devices based on weak artificial intelligence can only simulate this type of behavior, similar to that undertaken by humans. We thus see that both weak and strong artificial intelligence systems each have strengths and weaknesses (see Figure 2.1).

The last component of artificial intelligence is artificial superintelligence (ASI). In the professional literature, this term is often used with reference to the general and strong artificial intelligence at the point when it surpasses human intelligence as noticed by specialists from Accenture (2018), if this is ever to occur (see Figure 2.1). Therefore, it results from the definition above that artificial superintelligence has enormous potential, so far undefined in science or economy. It is mainly identified with the performance of tasks and works at

	Weak artificial intelligence	Strong artificial intelligence	Superintelligence
Definition	Weak artificial intelligence (*weak AI*) is based on the assumption that computer devices (machines) can simulate human intelligence, but without the need to demonstrate consciousness or be a thinking machine. For weak artificial intelligence, scientists use computers as tools to research the mind and not to build it (with related cognitive states).	Strong artificial intelligence (*strong AI*) is based on the assumption that computer devices (machines) can simulate human intelligence and, importantly, demonstrate consciousness. In addition, they will be thinking machines. For strong artificial intelligence, scientists use computers as tools to replicate the mind and reflect people's cognitive functions.	Artificial superintelligence (Artificial Super-Intelligence, ASI) is based on the assumption that the potential of computer devices (machines) will transcend people. For artificial superintelligence, scientists believe that a computer's cognitive abilities will be better than human ones.
Scope of potential and solutions	- logical thinking, - decision-making in the conditions of uncertainty, - possibility of planning, - possibility of learning, - communicating in natural language, - possibility of programming computers to think.	- navigation systems, - analytical systems and expert systems, - possibilities of creating a "real" world, - voice recognition, - character recognition, - speech recognition, - suggestions in searching for corrections and errors.	- digital Intelligence, - direct growth in speed of executed tasks and works, - ....? - ....?

Figure 2.1 Weak, strong and super artificial intelligence – comparative perspective. Source: Authors' own study on the basis of AiLab (2019) and Paschek et al. (2017).

speeds which are unavailable to humans (digital intelligence). It applies also to any activities that man, as a thinking creature, cannot perform despite the effort undertaken. In this context, a truly philosophical question arises: how smart is biological and synthetic intelligence? In reality, is it true that, without any doubt, we can conclude that synthetic beings will always be smarter than biological beings, in particular people? Any answer to such questions is not easy and, in the era of current scientific development, also. Everything seems to be dependent on the pace that AI, including artificial superintelligence, will develop in the years and decades to come. Experts from Oxford University and Stanford University are of the opinion that there is a 50 percent chance that over the next 45 years machines will surpass humanity in all tasks performed (Revell, 2017). On the other hand we have outstanding AI researchers who provide a contrary opinion and believe that in fact superintelligence will never materialize (Etzioni, 2016). Today it is difficult to say which group of scientists will be right. However, in the opinion of many experts, it is expected that artificial intelligence will master many activities earlier: by 2024 machines will be better than man in language translation, by 2026 they will have essay and school composition writing skills, by 2027 machines will drive trucks, by 2031 they will operate in retail trade, by 2049 they will have the skills of writing books including bestsellers, and by 2053 they will substitute a surgeon in the operating theater (Revell, 2017). In the context of the proposed dates and the resulting consequences for the labor market in particular and humanity in general, it seems appropriate to quote the British astrophysicist and cosmologist Stephen Hawking: “I am afraid that artificial intelligence could replace people completely”. In the opinion of this outstanding scholar, AI will be a new, previously unknown, form of life that will transcend people.

2.2 Basic elements of artificial intelligence – a classification

When considering the content of this chapter, initially it should be explained that we will consider as artificial intelligence elements any items that, simply put, create this intelligence. In practice, it is a set of various types of algorithms, systems, programs, models and techniques that all together and each separately bring into reality the concept of artificial intelligence. Considering its development stages (see Table 2.1), we notice that, decade after decade, not only the number of its forming elements is growing, but the level of their technological advancement is also increasing. As a result, humanity is presently fascinated by a new-generation humanoid robot from Japan, while not that long ago people were learning to operate the first Apple computers.

In subject literature, the description of the elements forming AI is quite scattered and diversified, probably a result of their number and multi-faceted nature. Therefore, to maintain order, in this chapter AI elements have been grouped into sections. Each of the three sections, in fact defined as phases, presents artificial intelligence elements with a breakdown by the degree of their technological advancement, which naturally correlates with its development stages (see

Table 2.1 Artificial intelligence – development stages

Year	Accompanying events
1940–1956	Birth of Artificial Intelligence
1950	Alan Turing test. The test was to determine whether the machine had mastered the natural language and whether it was possible for it to have thinking abilities like people. The test consisted in checking whether, within 5 minutes of a conversation, at least 30 percent of the interlocutors talking with the machine did not realize that they were not talking with a man.
1950	Isaac Asimov publishes the "Three Laws of Robotics". First Law: A robot may not injure a human being or, through inaction, allow a human being to come to harm. Second Law: A robot must obey the orders given it by human beings except where such orders would conflict with the First Law. Third Law: A robot must protect its own existence as long as such protection does not conflict with the First or Second Law.
1951	The first prototype of an artificial intelligence algorithm authored by Alan Turing is created.
1951	Marvin Lee Minsky builds the first stochastic neural network SNARC.
1952	American computer games pioneer Arthur Samuel, an IBM employee, develops the first self-learning checkers playing algorithm.
1955	John McCarthy coins the term "artificial intelligence".
1956	The first AI-dedicated conference at Dartmouth College.
1956–1974	The "Golden Age" of artificial intelligence
1959	The foundations for man–machine symbiosis are being created. The application of semantic networks by Margaret Masterman in theoretical and computer linguistics.
1960	Scientific teams involved in research on artificial intelligence from the universities in Stanford and Edinburgh begin work on the application of vision in robots.
1961	Installation of the first serial robot Unimate in the General Motors factory in Trenton, New Jersey. Growing popularity of Lisp, a high-level programing language.
1961	IBM Shoebox computer performs mathematical functions and recognizes speech.
1964	ELIZA is created in MIT artificial intelligence laboratory, an early computer software for the processing of natural language, authored by Joseph Weizenbaum.
1966	Shakey robot is created, the first general application mobile robot which was "aware" of its actions.
1967	Mac Hack is created, the first computer software for playing chess.
1972	Prolog is created, a logical programming language used for automatic natural language analysis.
1974	SHRDLU is created, an AI computer system for the processing of natural language.
	Creation of MYCIN Medical, an artificial intelligence software for the therapy of blood infections. The program diagnoses patients based on reported symptoms and medical test results.
	David Marr starts works on machine-based visual perception.
	Marvin Minsky's theory of frames is formulated.
1974–1980	Artificial intelligence "stagnation years"

(*Continued*)

Table 2.1 (Continued)

Year	*Accompanying events*
1979	Computer software defeated the world champion in Backgammon strategic game. For the first time the world champion had to admit the intellectual superiority of a man-created being.
1980–1987	Artificial intelligence “heyday years”
1980	Origins of parallel programing.
1982	Development of advanced machines (including, among others: R1,/ XCON) in industry which were to help salesforce to avoid errors while selling products.
1984	Development of neural networks, including error backpropagation algorithms.
1985	Ernst Dickmanns starts testing of a completely autonomous vehicle. First use of image processing technology in vehicles, with the application of innovative algorithms.
1987	Marvin Minsky’s design of artificial intelligence systems named “smart agents”.
1987–1994	Artificial intelligence “repeated stagnation years”
1988	Creation of ALVINN, a perception system learning to control vehicles on the basis of observations of the driving person.
1989	The first version of Chinook computer software for playing checkers is created.
1994–( )	“Contemporary times” in artificial intelligence
1996	Chess Grandmaster Garri Kasparov lost a game of chess with Deep Blue computer system.
1997	Chess Grandmaster Garri Kasparov lost a game of chess with Deeper Blue computer system (an improved Deep Blue version).
1999	First indexing robots are created.
1999	Development of semantic networks.
2000	Robopet is created (dog robot).
2000	Kismet is created, a program making it possible to detect wireless local networks.
2002	IRobot Roomba is created, a floor washing and care robot.
2004	World’s first autonomous vehicle championships (that is without drivers) – DARPA Grand Challenge.
2005	The first version of ASIMO is created, a Japanese humanoid robot created by Honda Motor Company.
2006	Start of Blue Brain Project – a Swiss brain research initiative with the aim of creating its digital version.
2010	Autonomous cars, without drivers.
2011	Creation of IBM Watson supercomputer, which wins Jeopardy quiz show.
2014	HRP-2 Promet is created, a Japanese humanoid robot created by Honda Motor Company.
2015	Market premiere of Google Alpha Go, a computer playing a board game.
2017	Google launches Google’s AutoML to the market, a software for automatic building and implementation of the most advanced machine learning models on structural data.
2019	Inventing artificial intelligence (player) for playing Texas Hold’em poker.

Source: Prepared by the authors on the basis of a literature review.

Table 2.1). In this way, we distinguish the following AI phases and elements (Boucher, 2019):

Phase I: symbolism-based artificial intelligence – these are the first, early, undeveloped AI elements, including:

- **expert systems** – according to the definition proposed by Edward Feigenbaum,[9] these are smart computer programs that use knowledge and reasoning procedures to solve problems with a high degree of complexity, stressing the necessity for an expert in the given domain to solve the problem. In other words, the point is to acquire knowledge from an expert and transfer it to the computer program. In expert systems, problems are solved by reasoning with the use of any possessed knowledge resources, and not conventional procedural codes. The first expert systems were built in the 1970s, and then, on a larger scale, were popularized in the 1980s.
- **fuzzy logic** – a theory developed in the 1970s by Lotfi A. Zadeh.[10] Fuzzy logic is based on an observation that people make decisions based on imprecise and non-numerical information. In practice we often use not very precise notions, e.g. a bit, much, above, significantly, which cannot be assigned any specific values and which cannot be qualified to a specific set of or subset of characteristics. Fuzzy logic is particularly useful in engineering-based design and implementation of algorithms, as part of creating AI. At present, home equipment elements, e.g. household articles, are described by the words "*fuzzy logic inside*", meaning that control of the processes inside these devices proceeds with the use of elements of the fuzzy set theory.
- **evolutionary algorithms** – algorithms based on Darwin's theory of evolution which are an attempt to take advantage of the evolution mechanisms known from nature to solve optimization problems. An evolutionary algorithm works through a selection process where poorly adapted individuals are eliminated from the population, while better adapted ones have an opportunity to survive. In practice evolutionary algorithms are nothing other than computer applications that resemble biological processes for solving complex problems.

Phase II: data set-based artificial intelligence – a set of AI elements, the usability and innovative operation of which are based on processing large information silos. In other words, algorithms, related e.g. to machine learning, are subject to a self-improvement process, thanks to being "trained" on databases. In this phase, among the basic AI elements we can distinguish:

- **artificial neural networks and deep learning**. At present, artificial neural networks have a broad range of applications in many areas of science. However, they are most often identified with the technical aspects related to image compression, identification and reemission. The operation of artificial neural networks is based on the functionalities of the electro-chemical neural networks in the brains of both people and animals. Simply put, the point is to transfer and change incentive signals, as a result of them going through complex networks of human or animal neurons. In the case of deep learning, it is a complex process where the computer learns how to perform tasks that are natural for the human brain. They mainly apply to speech recognition, image identification or forecasting techniques. In the case of deep learning, the computer collects basic parameters concerning the data and gets organized for individual learning, through identification of paradigms with the application of many processing layers.

- **error backpropagation algorithm** – an algorithm determining the procedure (that is the manner of calculating) the correction of weights in multi-layer networks with the use of the so-called gradient-based optimization methods.[11] In other words, the error backpropagation algorithm is one of the most effective ones, and it is used for training feed-forwarded, multi-layer neural networks. At the same time it should be noted that the flow of information in the network proceeds one way. It is also worth mentioning that this algorithm gained popularity in the second half of the 1980s, when we understood[12] that it operates much faster in neural networks than the earlier learning process approaches. In consequence, this allowed neural networks to be used to solve problems that were earlier considered unsolvable. At present, this algorithm is perceived as the "workhorse" of the learning process in neural networks.
- **speech recognition** – an AI element where the computer or another device identifies spoken words. In fact, it is natural language recognition in the verbal form. In this way, users can control digital devices using audio commands instead of using conventional tools, such as a keyboard, a mouse, or a touchpad.
- **voice recognition** – is possible using software that operates with the application of sound and language modeling algorithms. Acoustic modeling relies on a combination of language units and audio signals, while language modeling is based on the adjustment of sounds to the sequence of words being spoken, in order to distinguish between those that sound similar.
- **image recognition** – one of those AI elements which, with the use of computer technologies, can recognize particular persons, animals, items or other objects thanks to the algorithms used and the machine learning concept. It is worth mentioning that image identification is related to the vision of the computer, which allows it not only to learn, but also to see people and process images, which, for the computer is essentially intensive work on data concerning a particular object. Many techniques used for image recognition require the use of perceptron neural networks for filtering images through a number of artificial neuron layers.
- **data mining** – the process of discovering generalized rules and knowledge contained in databases, based on quantitative (mathematical, statistical) methods and artificial intelligence techniques.
- **intelligent agent** – an artificial intelligence element which refers to an autonomous (independent) being that is focused on achieving specific goals. An intelligent agent can be a computer, robot or another device (but also a man),

which, using sensors (including, among others: cameras, mobile phones, infrared radiation) perceives and influences the surrounding environment through an executive module (actuator). In practice, a software agent can independently operate on input data or display them on the screen, provided that the actuator is pressed or switched on.

Phase III: superintelligence-based artificial intelligence – a set of AI elements the technology of which is not limited to, say, a specific scope or set of algorithms, but works intelligently in a broad range of circumstances and problem spaces. In fact, superintelligent elements become smart and autonomous enough to generate even more intelligent and autonomous artificial intelligence. Owing to the fact that the artificial superintelligence concept is an undertaking which today does not give any guarantee that it will ever materialize, its component parts as described below are rather concerned with the potential and the development directions than a technology that will be commonly used "tomorrow". Therefore, the following may become elements of artificial superintelligence:

- **robotic artificial intelligence** – is characterized by the fact that a model of the environment in which the robot is staying is created in the first place, and then a number of alternative strategies are considered to achieve a certain result based on this model. Then, from among the analyzed strategies, implementation occurs for the optimal one from the point of view of achieving the desired outcome. Such an approach to robotic artificial intelligence is today in clear contrast to the currently operated reactive systems that define the robot's environment first, and then record its initially coded behaviors.
- **quantum artificial intelligence** – an interdisciplinary area of activities that focuses on building quantum algorithms in order to improve computational "abilities" in the area of artificial intelligence. In fact, it is based on the opportunity to use quantum computers for further development of quantum artificial intelligence, which will further AI development. At present, the whole concept related to quantum reinforcement of artificial intelligence algorithms is still in the phase of conceptual works.
- **brain emulation** – a process consisting in copying or transferring the human consciousness to the computer. In practice, this concept assumes creating a computer program whose attributes would reflect the retention of human personality. Currently the technology of modeling the human brain based on intact computer thoughts and feelings, memories, dreams or skills, remains rather in the domain of science fiction literature.
- **artificial consciousness** – often referred to as machine consciousness, computer consciousness, synthetic consciousness or artificial beings' consciousness. Its naming aside, it is an attempt to model and implement those aspects of human cognition that are identified with the idea, frequently presented as elusive and controversial, regarding the phenomenon of brain consciousness (Saxena & Gopal, 2013). Importantly, the point here is not really to reproduce human consciousness as such (namely one to one), because its

complexity, determined by cultural, social and biological aspects seems to overwhelm even the greatest contemporary thinkers. Although not only from a scientific point of view, artificial consciousness modeling seems to be extremely interesting, computer scientists, nanotechnologists and neurobiologists agree on that many problems identified in this area are yet to be solved, for artificial consciousness and emulation of the whole brain to be feasible at all. Therefore, at present, we can only consider these concepts as theoretical technologies.

- **wetware and biological systems** – are concepts related to "artificial life", differing from artificial intelligence in that the ideas are based on fundamental biological processes and not intelligence or expert knowledge. In practice, wetware means any equipment (hardware) or software systems (software) with a biological component (wetware), which operate as a regular computer. Simply put, one can say that, in this concept, biological materials are used as elements to create new computer software. The potential of wetware application (wetware) seems to be particularly high in such domains as: bioengineering, genetic research, synthetic biology or medical neuro-engineering.

To end this section, it must be concluded that the above described artificial intelligence elements are undoubtedly the fundamental and most important ones. This does not mean that they exhaust the topic, as present in literature, especially since the number of AI-forming elements is growing rather than decreasing, a situation caused by the sustained interest in the artificial intelligence area among scientists, inventors and entrepreneurs. In addition, year after year, AI forming elements "demonstrate" a higher level of technological advancement, which should be correlated directly with the AI development phases over the last several decades. Clearly, this process is continuing, so within AI we are dealing with better and better concepts, techniques, models, systems and algorithms, to the extent that a question arises about the limits of this "extremely" human-like level of artificial intelligence. A reflection in this regard also seems necessary: the world of artificial intelligence unquestionably is not only a world of real opportunities but also real threats. We do not want to only worry about them, but quickly identify and continuously monitor them. In practice, a good model for such an approach is the Future of Life Institute (FLI)[13] established in Cambridge (USA) in 2014, whose activities focus on limiting the existential risks humanity is exposed to in the context of further advanced development of artificial intelligence.

2.3 Impact of artificial intelligence on business and the economy

It is difficult to deny the fact that our life and global socio-economic development are increasingly dependent upon artificial intelligence. Its development in the fields of medicine, technology, engineering, psychology, economy or astronomy is dynamic enough to conclude that we are presently living in the **artificial intelligence era**. AI development in the global economy has been possible due to a combination of three different, though interrelated, changes (Ernst et al., 2018):

- first, the phenomenon of a sharp decline in computation costs that in practice has translated into the growth in the machines' computational power and their memory capacity. As a result, even the simplest smartphone models are presently more efficient than a computer[14] that took the first man to the Moon. Another good example may be the cost of producing a series 7 iPhone. Currently it oscillates around USD 220–240 per unit, while in the 1980s, mostly due to memory card capacities, the manufacturing cost would amount to almost USD 1.2 million. This means that presently such phone production costs are more than 5000 times lower than they would have been in the 1980s,
- second, the development and broad application of the Internet and other forms of digital communication, which have led to an extraordinary growth in the supply of digital information storage. At the same time, thanks to computational cloud services, already discussed earlier, companies can analyze and compare significant amounts of data for statistical and stochastic purposes, which are necessary to develop tools (applications) based on AI principles,
- third, significant capital cost reductions in digital technologies that have led to a reduction in the market entry barriers for new companies. In reality, various types of startups have strongly benefited from this development, as today they do not have to engage large amounts of capital to start a new project. Furthermore, the perhaps unprecedented development of digital technology has questioned the Uppsala internationalization model, which assumes sequential company transition through subsequent stages in the internationalization process, as presently, for a company to became global, it just needs to have access to the Internet.[15] However, we should not forget that changes of business models, benefiting small and rapidly developing technological firms, originated from the academic community at many universities, where the world of business combined its experience with the world of science by creating spin-off companies.

The changes presented above, which became the driving force in the global development of artificial intelligence, led to its perception as the main determinant of economic growth worldwide. This thesis seems to be confirmed by the results of research conducted by Accenture (Purdy & Daugherty, 2016), which, in terms of the effect of AI on economic growth similar to the GDP (namely, Real Gross Value Added, GVA), analyzed the economies of 12 developed countries including the United States, Finland, the UK, Sweden, the Netherlands, Germany, Austria, France, Japan, Belgium, Spain and Italy (see Figure 2.2).

In this context it turns out that almost all of the analyzed countries that will use AI in the economy can double their annual GDP growth by 2035. The same forecasts, in the opinion of Accenture experts, also apply to the growth rate in the global economy. Importantly, economic growth will be driven by artificial intelligence in three principal ways (Szczepański, 2019). First, solutions involving AI are to lead, thanks to their technological innovation, to a geometric growth in work efficiency. It is anticipated that an improvement in this respect may reach as much as 40 percent of what is available at present. The growth in work efficiency

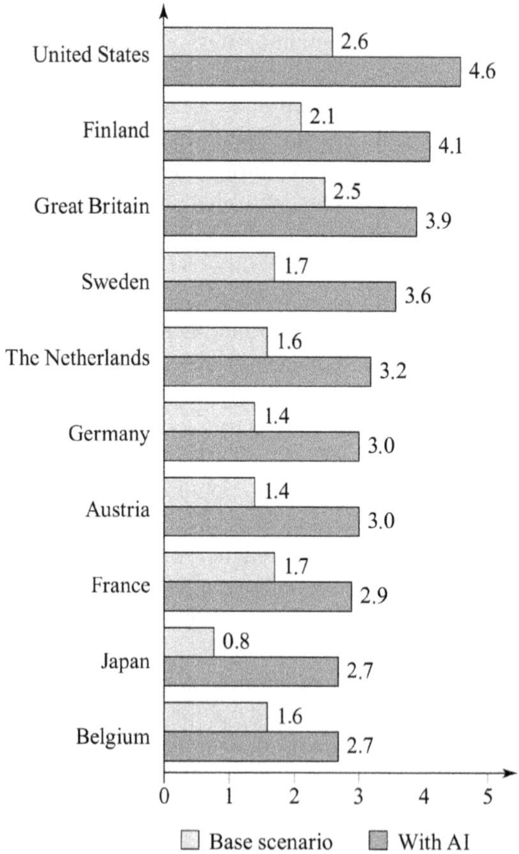

Figure 2.2 Annual pace of gross added value (Real Gross Value Added, GVA) in 2035 (similar to GDP) comparing growth in 2035 according to the base scenario and a scenario assuming AI utilization in the economy (as a percent). Source: Purdy and Daughert (2016).

is specifically due to better management of the time related to work employment and organization. Second, AI will create a new, virtual workforce in the form of intelligent automation. In practice, this will be a digital application, able to solve problems and self-learn, in fact collaborating with and not replacing man. Third, the economy will be "growing" thanks to the advantages from dissemination of innovations, which, affecting different sectors, will create new, additional sources of income. Similar research was also conducted by specialists from PwC[16] (Gillham et al., 2018). This time their calculations were based on the S-CGE[17] model, which served to evaluate the net effect of artificial intelligence on the global economy until 2030. PwC research demonstrated that, thanks to coupling AI into world economic circulation, by 2030 the global GDP level can increase by as much as 14 percent, compared to 2018. In practice, what is emphasized by expert is that this will account for nearly USD 16 trillion in additional contributions to the development of the global economy. Interestingly, PwC experts, as in the case of Accenture specialists, also think that artificial intelligence will drive GDP growth mostly by improvements in aspects related to efficiency of work and manufacturing processes, introduction of intelligent automation or by increasing consumer demand. In the latter case, its level will, above all, result from the growing availability of highly personalized products and services, created as a result of using AI. Over the years the consumption of high quality goods itself can, in the opinion of PwC experts, be subject to a significant increase through, among others, the network effect,[18] making its nominal contribution to global GDP growth by 2030 exceed one resulting solely from growth in the efficiency measure. Thus, the networking effects mentioned here create tremendous possibilities in particular for those companies that are perceived by the market and the world of business as artificial intelligence leaders, whose solutions and products presently determine the strength of national economies in particular, and the global economy in general (see Table 2.2). However, what is also worth noting, their favorable position overshadows other companies that have problems with the absorption of artificial intelligence-based solutions, putting them in an unfavorable competitive position. Consequently, at the global level, disequilibria are growing in this area, characteristic for those technologies or concepts that develop extremely dynamically. To confirm these words, it is enough to note that the vast majority of AI companies come from China, North America and Europe, while a small number are from Africa, Latin America, South America, Oceania and Asia. A similar geographical distribution occurs with the amount of investment expenses particular countries spend on artificial intelligence-related technology development.

Bearing in mind the above, we see that worldwide fast development of artificial intelligence, alongside a number of opportunities, creates many real problems. This should make us ask difficult but relevant questions, including one concerning the general system of social (collective) accountability for the further development of AI worldwide. In other words, the point is to develop commonly accepted methods which will protect consumers from digital exclusion, offer incentives to companies to create and deliver technologically safe products and services, remove barriers that slow down and hinder humanity's further development as well as create possibilities for innovative and continuous development, in particular for those least economically developed regions of the world.

Although there is a real concern that the development of artificial intelligence will deepen development-related disparities in the modern world, in many developing or poorly developed countries it is perceived as a technology that can actually change their present economic situation. It should be mentioned that, from the technological point of view, devices, machines, applications or systems utilizing artificial intelligence are often based on low-cost solutions, and therefore they are available to a wide group of users. As an example, we can mention countless applications, which facilitate daily functioning of contemporary people and which can be downloaded through a mobile phone, at no cost. Furthermore, some

Table 2.2 Leading companies in AI sphere with applications affecting the market and the economy

Company	*Technology/platform*	*AI applications with a significant effect on the market and the economy*	*Solutions such as open source*
Amazon	• A computing cloud • Online retail sale services • Electronic appliances	• **Alexa:** virtual AI assistant. • **Amazon AI platform:** is cloud software and AI tools.	• **Deep Scalable Sparse Tensor Network Engine (DSSTNE):** is a library for creating models in the machine learning and deep learning area.
Apple Inc.	• A manufacturer of computers, electronic appliances and software manufacturer • Online services	• **Siri:** a smart personal system which uses solutions involving AI. • **Autonomous cars:** is an AI technology allowing driving a car without the human interaction.	• **Swift:** a tool within open source for writing apps in swift language. It is a general application programming language.
Facebook	• Social media site	• **Applied Machine Learning:** is an application which is used to develop a learning system in order to solve a particular type problem, also in the learning area. • **Human Computer Interaction (HCI):** is design of a computer technology focused on interactions between people (users) and computers. Within HCI, it is possible to describe, using a computer, images for blind users.	• **CommAI-env:** communication-based platform for training and evaluation of AI systems. • **fbcunn:** deep learning modules for graphic processing units (GPU).
Google DeepMind	• Search engines, maps, advertisements, gmail, android, chrome and youtube.	• **Autonomous cars:** is an advanced technology, which allows cars to move in regular road traffic without any control from the man (driverless cars).	• **TensorFlow:** open source programming library (frequently considered as the best) mostly used by beginners and experts in machine learning and neural networks.
	• Deep Q-Network (DQN): deep neural networks with reinforcement learning (RL).	**AlphaGo:** is the first computer software, which defeated professional players in the old Chinese board game Go. • **DQN:** is better than human control of ATARI games by deep, reinforcement learning (DRL). • **WaveNet:** is a system creating language models (raw sounds).	• **DeepMind Lab:** is a game-like 3D platform applicable in studies on AI, based on the so-called agents. • **Sonnet:** a program used for building deep neural networks on the basis of TensorFlow library.

IBM	• Computer and software manufacturer • Hosting and consulting services • Smart data processing	• **Deep(er) Blue:** the first computer software that defeated a chess Grandmaster. • **Watson:** a supercomputer created to answer questions in "Jeopardy" popular quiz show, which wins this quiz show with the best result in history.	• **Apache SystemML:** an application that provides an optimal workplace for machine learning with the use of large data collections. • **Apache UIMA:** is an application which is used to manage a large amount of unstructured information, in order to discover knowledge for the end user.
Microsoft	• Development, production as well as licensing of computer hardware and software • Electronic appliances	• **Microsoft Azure:** is an open and flexible corporate class cloud computing platform. It allows access to mechanisms allowing data processing and storage. • **Cortana:** a virtual assistant based on AI algorithms. In practice, it can integrate with a large number of other Windows system applications.	• **Microsoft Azure:** a platform for smart data processing that is offered as a service. • **The Microsoft Cognitive Toolkit (CNTK):** is an open source tool, used for deep learning.
Open AI	• Non-profit organizations • Evolutionary algorithms • Deep neural networks	• **Evolutionary algorithms:** are algorithms that are adapted to working with deep neural networks. • **Testbeds for AI:** are tools (the so-called testbed), which serve software designers for comparative tests and efficiency measures for AI algorithms.	• **Gym:** is a set of tools for the development and comparison of RL algorithms. • **Universe:** a platform with software used to measure and develop AI in the world of games, websites, and other applications.

Source: Own study based on Perez et al. (2017).

manufacturers are still willing to pay for the mere fact of using them, refunding small amounts to the user's bank account e.g. cashback after shopping made in the selected store. Going further, we also know that many of the **expert systems**[19] based on artificial intelligence can be activated from the level of mobile phones, which has facilitated their popularity among users in poor, poorly developed or developing countries (Ernst et al., 2018). Therefore, in many tech companies across the world, expert systems are presently being developed to help small and very small agricultural farms to obtain better information on what, when and how to plant or sow to increase yields. Some solutions from this area already operate on the market and are used by farmers from African countries. Here, an example can be of certain semi-desert regions in Africa, where information obtained from expert systems on meteorological conditions, cultivation techniques and methods and irrigation methods has led to a growth in the potential and actual yields, thanks to the application of proper seeds and water savings (Ernst et al., 2018). In practice, such solutions create great opportunities for everybody employed in the agricultural sector.

It is also an excellent opportunity to ensure better development and increase income for poor and poorly developed countries, whose economies are often based on agriculture, or countries where this sector accounts for a significant share in the national GDP. We thus see that the development of AI also, and perhaps first of all, in agriculture has a bright future which can prove essential particularly for economies in poor and developing countries. AI-based agricultural systems carry huge potential, for example in the area of creating **weather models**. Their design is based on the analysis of collected weather data, quantities of water in soil and in the air, the level of nitrogen, air quality or recognition of plant diseases, which are then sent to a computational cloud. Then, in the cloud they are juxtaposed with information from previous periods. In this manner, subject to additional support from the GPS system, extremely precise weather models are created, which are able not only to forecast and take advantage of weather in agriculture, but also to prevent loss of any effort often involved in cultivation. Expert systems can also be used, e.g. to reduce transport and logistics costs. This solution seems particularly important for manufacturers in developing countries, where access to large distribution networks is very limited.

In the context of the topic addressed here, the last example worth mentioning is the use of AI-based expert systems by decision-makers, particularly in countries with limited fiscal resources (Ernst et al., 2018). In practice, the execution of public tasks often depends on timely and precise information on any areas requiring intervention and this "type" of information is offered by expert systems, allowing authorities to better manage interventions or crisis situations. It is a solution also proven effective in health care management, especially in countries continuously facing epidemics, wars and poverty.

To end this section, it will not be an exaggeration to observe that the impact AI development will have on the economy and society, will most likely be the largest one humanity has ever experienced. The three previous industrial revolutions have primarily reevaluated our approach to manufacturing, whereas the fourth one, related to artificial intelligence, will reevaluate our approach to our entire life.[20] It is beyond doubt that the impact of AI solutions on us, but also on national economies, will be sequential, and we will be able to observe the effects better after some time. However, in the case of the economy, many experts already believe that artificial intelligence not only contributes to economic growth but can also be perceived as a completely new production factor. When it comes to the AI developmental trend itself, here many experts also agree that its form will reflect an S-like curve.[21]

2.4 Artificial intelligence 2.0 – the evolutionary development path

At present, it is difficult to come across anyone who has never heard about artificial intelligence. In the world of science and research, this concept, had been developed since the early 1950s (see Table 2.1 and Table 2.3). In practice, this means that its present "shape" or level of development is essentially a result of the examinations, analyses and concepts developed in the AI domain across 70 years. The origins of its development can be called embryonic, when the first concepts, tests, research and inventions were born, related to IT systems' abilities to correctly interpret data from the external environment (from outside of the system). This period, also defined in the subject literature as **Artificial Intelligence 0.5 (AI 0.5)** (see Table 2.3), was characterized by not only the first successes and discoveries but also the first failures, e.g. the first studies on robots or smart computers were disappointing from the point of view of science in general, and AI in particular, and did not contribute any real value to the further development of AI other than additional experiences. After this period, the first AI wave arrived, also referred to as **Artificial Intelligence 1.0 (AI 1.0)**. It started in the early 1980s and lasted for 15 years, approximately until 1995. From a scientific, but also practical perspective, it was mainly characterized by a great acceleration in the development of multi-layer neural networks (earlier simple stochastic neural networks, authored by Marvin Minsky – see Table 2.3) and the development of artificial intelligence applications in different areas of life. In addition, humanity witnessed the first, commercial applications of AI elements in various types of ventures, including those related to the automotive industry and the development of autonomous vehicles. Furthermore, that period was also the era of development and commercialization of technologies related to language and object-oriented programming, expert systems or deep neural networks, including the error back-propagation algorithms.[22] The first AI wave was characterized by the fact that systems or applications built at that time were made manually. It was quite simple, when compared to contemporary times: computer programmers, when solving often complex problems, transformed their ideas into codes and mathematical algorithms, which were later uploaded to systems and machines. As a result, they were able to solve various predefined problems that humanity was facing on a daily basis. Therefore, owing to its simplicity and "archaism" at the same time, AI from that period is often colloquially referred to as the Good Old-Fashioned

Table 2.3 Artificial intelligence from 0.5 to 3.0 – stages of development

Stages	*Accompanying events*
Artificial Intelligence 0.5: birth of AI, first research and inventions.	First intelligence test – Turing Test (1950) Beginning of research in machine learning: • Marvin Minsky's first stochastic neural network (1951), • construction of the first, simplest neural network, the perceptron by Frank Rosenblatt and Charles Wightman (1957–1959). First use of the term "Artificial Intelligence" and organization, for the first time in the world, of a conference devoted to AI in Dartmouth College (1955–1956). John McCarthy's creation of the first, basic programming language LISP (1958). Bruce Buchanan, Edward Feigenbaum and Joshua Lederberg develop the first expert system named DENDRAL, a precursor of expert systems (1965). Turing Test and natural language processing with the use of ELIZA, a psychotherapist simulator (1966). The first humanoid robot WABOT-1 created by Waseda University, Tokyo. The robot consisted of a system of extremities, a vision system and a conversation system. It could communicate in the Japanese language and measure distances and directions from other objects by means external receptors, artificial ears, eyes and lips (1970–1973). Marvin Minsky's and Seymour Papert's research confirms perceptron restrictions, in consequence a deadlock begins, lasting more than a decade, in the works on artificial neural networks and AI (1969).
Artificial Intelligence 1.0: further research on AI development, its first commercial applications. Creating expert systems and the hardware infrastructure for the operation of AI.	The first commercial application of expert systems, including e.g. PROSPECTOR, R1, XCON (1980). Specialist (music) humanoid robot WABOT-2 created by Waseda University, Tokyo. The robot could communicate in the Japanese language, read music scores, play medium difficulty melodies on electronic organs, accompany a person listening to another, singing person. The construction of WABOT-2 paved the way for the further development of personal robots (1980–1984). Development of projects on the construction of 5 generation robots (1982). Development and commercialization of LISP technology of machines, general purpose computers (1979–1985).

(*Continued*)

Table 2.3 (Continued)

Stages	*Accompanying events*
	Development of Object-Oriented Programming (OOP): C++, Object Pascal, Java, C#, etc. (1980). Further development of expert systems, including e.g.: EMYCIN, ART, KEE, OPS5, Nexpert Object, etc. (1980–1989) Development of deep neural networks, including error backpropagation algorithms (1984). 1980s beginning of weapon manufacturers' intensive research, mostly in the United States, on the application of AI in autonomous vehicles, battle management systems or military aviation. Stagnation years in AI development (1987-1994).
Artificial Intelligence 2.0: accelerated development of multi-layer neural networks, a significant growth in the application of AI solutions in different aspects of life.	AI development driven by the technology of processing and analyzing large heterogeneous databases. It is based on the use of paradigm recognition or deep, machine learning-related concepts (1999 –....). Development of the innovative *internet crowd intelligence* concept that involves problems solving with the help of "crowd intelligence", obtained by collection and deep analysis of intelligence data (2005). Development of *cross-media intelligence* idea (2013). Creating hybrid human-machine intelligence. Works on augmented intelligence (*human-machine hybrid-augmented intelligence*) (2005). Development of smart autonomous vehicles (2000).
Artificial Intelligence 3.0?: development of general artificial intelligence, works on artificial human brain.	Works on the technology of neuromorphic CPUs imitating the functioning of the human brain (2010). IBM Watson is created, a cognitive supercomputer developed by IBM (2011). Production of TrueNorth, a neuromorphic integrated system – Exmor CMOS (2014). Launch of a neuromorphic system, called *Loihi*, by Intel, designed based on the human brain. Construction of parallel neuromorphic computer devices that are modeled after the nervous tissue (203.?). ....?

Source: Authors' own study.

Artificial Intelligence (GOFAI). Although the period of Artificial Intelligence 1.0, as compared to 0.5, clearly featured a more dynamic and accelerated development, it still did not manage to avoid the period of "scientific stagnation", which in this case took place at the turn of the 1980s and 1990s.

The years of stagnation in AI development should not, however, be perceived as a deep inertia, but rather as a period when research on AI was weak and did not exert any significant effect on its development. The early 1990s were characterized by commercialization and a growing popularity of the Internet, especially due to its privatization, conducted in the United States in 1992. As a result, the number of private Internet suppliers and domestic websites increased dramatically, changing marketing and commerce forever. Those events were accompanied by the dynamic development of various types of sensors (including optical, process or, in recent years, biomedical) and large data collections, combined with their analysis (big data). Furthermore, e-trade took on new meaning, proof of which can be seen in the number of transactions presently made through the Amazon.com platform.[23] A similar situation occurred in the development of the information society under which infosphere and sociosphere areas have achieved unprecedented growth, and information itself is currently perceived by countries as a basic resource and a fundamental economic category. In consequence, progress of world development, occurring through the above-described events and accompanied by mutual penetration of the growing amounts of information as well as knowledge in both physical and cyber-physical space, resulted in AI also being subject to evolution. Its increasing omnipresence and offering of smart and highly personalized products to customers make our times the era of **Artificial Intelligence 2.0 (AI 2.0)**. The principal causal factors that determine its development are (Pan, 2016):

- first, the development of the 21st-century information environment, which is subject to extremely dynamic transformations related to the popularity of mobile devices, the Internet, and an extensive network of various types of sensors, devices as well as vehicles. In addition, many cities around the world already use, for the purposes of management or security, universal devices detecting the presence of people, machines and vehicles on streets, squares or in municipal zones. Also, the fast development of networks connecting people across the globe, which has never happened before on this scale, is a reflection and simultaneously harmonizes the requirements, knowledge and experience that are offered by the contemporary world. Importantly, we can also conclude that the world has evolved from a binary space, based on physics and society, into a ternary space, based on physics, society, but also virtual reality. As a result, the interactions present in the ternary space create new computational paradigms, which are later applied in areas related to broadly defined perception, taxonomy, augmented reality or cross-media computing,
- second, the continuously growing demand for further development of artificial intelligence, including products and services employing its elements and solutions. An effect of this is insistence on scientific research (see Table 2.4) concerning this topic, the scale and pace of which are additionally motivated by the requirements formulated in the AI sphere from outside the academic community. In other words, the idea is also to actively promote research on AI among entrepreneurs, who see it as a source of methods for solving problems in the contemporary world of medicine, transport, production, logistics, the automotive sector or modern technologies,

Table 2.4 Research on the development of artificial intelligence 2.0 and artificial general intelligence – a literature review

Subject matter of research literature	*Author/source*
Development of a hybrid, synergistic platform (system) *Tianjic*, supporting further development of general artificial intelligence (AGI). In fact, it is a concept of merging, previously separated, incompatible AGI platforms, artificial neural networks based on information technology with models and algorithms built on the basis of neurobiology.	(Pei et al., 2019)
Research on new areas used to test the consciousness of machines (utilization of the consciousness theory in the development of AI 2.0) on the basis of an internal measurement called *Pak Pandir test*. The test utilizes a triple setting of a double quantum slot and the information integration theory, in this way defines the selection of the consciousness.	(Nazri et al., 2018)
Preparation of the concept of using the video games environment in research on artificial intelligence. The authors, in order to improve research in this area and within cognitive sciences recommend the application of *StarCraft II Learning Environment*, in order to perform man–machine tests and studies (artificial agents).	(Siljebrít et al., 2018)
The authors reviewed the latest developments in artificial intelligence, from the point of view of both theory and practice, considering the matters related to big data companies. In the conclusion of their studies they stated that integrated machine learning based on human knowledge may effectively ensure achievement of solid, general artificial intelligence.	(Zhuang et al., 2017)
The authors described collective social intelligence concepts (Crowd Intelligence, CI) and explained its relationships with other existing ideas, e.g. crowdsourcing (the practice of involving the "crowd" for a shared, often innovative, goal) or calculations based on the human being (Human-Based Computation, HBC). In addition, the authors developed four categories of representative platforms within collective social (crowd) intelligence.	(Li et al., 2017)
The scientists reviewed the latest research in the area of perception, including visual perception, auditory perception and speech perception. Apart from that, they also analyzed the matters related to works on processing information and learning mechanisms.	(Tian et al., 2017)
The authors set out new trends in the development of smart, unmanned autonomous systems used in vehicles, aircraft, service robots, space robots, sea robots.	(Zhang et al., 2017)
The authors proposed an approach to effectively untangle any discriminating characteristics by the common utilization of the "crowd" wisdom and deep learning for the task related to the named entity disambiguation (NED).	(Zhou et al., 2017)
Development of a multi-sensor focused on vision for the perception of the road traffic environment for autonomous driving systems, which, through a set of data delivered e.g. through a video camera, helps the vehicle to self-localize and avoid obstacles.	(Xue et al., 2017)

Source: Prepared by the authors based on e.g. Pan (2017).

- third, great changes, to which AI has been subjected to over the last several decades, which in fact have "resulted" in a transition from the regular use of a computer to treating it as a simulator of human intelligence. This transformation made it possible to significantly improve smart hybrid systems connecting machines and people, create new collective social intelligence systems on the basis of machines, people and networks (see Table 2.4) and build complex systems in the form of e.g. smart cities, where human factors and social factors intertwine with the world of physics and cyberspace,
- and fourth, modification of artificial intelligence-related data resources. It is necessary to mention that the development of algorithms for processing large amounts of data, often coming from various sources, creates in fact a new information environment for AI. At the same time, new algorithms (including evolutionary or biological ones), data warehouses, networks of connections and sensors will determine the unavoidable trend that the development of AI will follow in the years to come.

The factors discussed above were not only the driving force in the development of the second AI wave (because this is also how the concept of AI 2.0 is defined in the literature), but they have contributed to technological progress in its area. In this context, it is worth paying attention to several new and interesting ideas that are a realization of the AI 2.0 concept (Pan, 2016). The first is concerned with big-data-based AI. In practice this solution allows for transformation of large quantities of data available into useful and specific knowledge. The second, innovative idea refers to solving problems with the help of internet crowd intelligence. An example of the application of this concept can be the *Zhihu* platform, which is a Q&A (Questions & Answers) knowledge base available for Chinese society. Since its creation in 2011, it has reached more than 110 million answers. According to *Zhihu*[24] data, more than 70 percent of the platform users are persons who are looking for professional knowledge and are participants in the self-improvement process. The third concept concerns cross-media intelligence. At present, it is an active research area in the field of information technology and a promising direction in further AI development. In the broad perspective, its operation centers on the use of information obtained from different forms of perception (including vision, language, hearing) in the form of text, images, voice or video recordings to perform tasks related to identification, reasoning, designing, creating, anticipating and programming. The integration of perception forms and the media[25] allows recognition of the external environment in which a particular machine operates. The fourth of the solutions is determined as human–machine hybrid augmented intelligence. In this case, the point is to create smart models that require human interaction to function properly. Creating such systems significantly strengthens general artificial intelligence, which already surpasses human intelligence in some areas (see Figure 2.3). At present, man–machine hybrid augmented intelligence systems are applicable, for example, in driving unmanned vehicles or in designing bionic skeletons (exoskeletons). The fifth and last of the initiatives, is concerned with

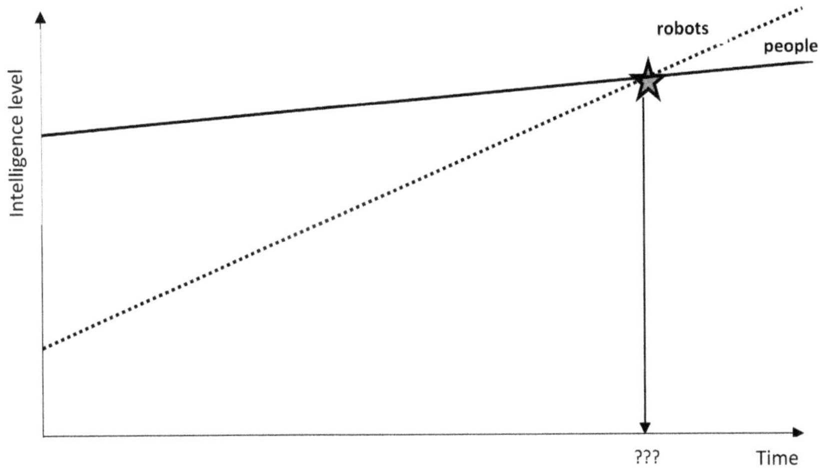

Figure 2.3 When will the level of robot intelligence exceed the level of human intelligence?
Source: https://natemat.pl/blogi/ryszardtadeusiewicz/154453,kiedy-roboty-stana-sie-madrzejsze-od-ludzi. Downloaded: 10.10.2019.

autonomous-intelligent systems. Because progress in artificial intelligence significantly exceeds that in robotics, at present AI elements are the driving force in the design and development of unmanned combat vehicles, aircraft or sea vessels. It can even be concluded that, through the development visible in smart autonomous systems, the unmanned element has reached out to almost every area of life where it can only be applicable.

The technologies described above are a new stage in the global development of artificial intelligence. Its "second wave" is a new generation of products and services featuring greater "intelligence", greater "intuition" and greater "knowledge". These are the things that connect and integrate, within their structures, machine learning, deep learning or deep neural network approaches with methods based on perception and knowledge. It is highly probable that over several years AI 2.0 will progress further in the area of hybrid augmented intelligence, development of the collective social intelligence as well as in the improvement of smart autonomous systems. In practice, a change for the better in these areas will probably change the present shape of cities, products, services, economy, environment and entire societies. Bearing this in mind, it might seem that AI 2.0 has not reached its heyday phase yet but is rather at a precursor stage. Meanwhile, first comments emerge now in the literature, indicating that the works related to neuromorphic CPUs imitating the functioning of the human brain or creation of the first cognitive supercomputers should be considered a manifestation of not the second, but already the third wave of artificial intelligence (AI 3.0) (see Table 2.3). AI 3.0 is a concept, which, unlike previous ones, will be distinguished by more complicated and at the same time more complex systems and solutions. AI

3.0 architecture is cognitive intelligence, which perhaps will be able to explain to us how the modern world functions.

2.5 Artificial intelligence development prospects in the economy

Contrary to what one can imagine, artificial intelligence is no longer a fashion or a temporary trend, but a reality, and also a virtual, reality. Although the discussion about AI, both in the scientific and business communities, has continued for a few decades, one can presently get an impression, a correct one, that it has grown in strength. Thus, a question arises about the origins of this surge in humanity's interest in the problem area related to fuzzy logic, evolutionary computations, neural networks, "artificial life", humanoid robots or self-learning systems. Its foundation is extremely important since we are dealing with a complex matter, not an easy subject of schemes or logical reasoning. Yet the answer to this question does not seem to be complicated – "something" that so far has been perceived by a significant majority in futuristic terms of a vision of the world, is beginning to materialize. Moreover, this process not only occurs before the eyes of hundreds of millions of people, but they also are its most important element, being the final buyer of products and services offered by AI technology. Thus, everything that is new, revealing and tangible raises a deep interest among a broad group of users.

Entrepreneurs and producers focus their attention on artificial intelligence in a special way, as more and more of them participate in the global race related to AI. The stakes seem to be high enough that the states that are currently building their economic potential on AI will have a clearly higher GDP in the years to come than those that have not taken up this challenge: the more so in that, across their territories, annual investment in AI product development is already counted in billions of US dollars. Importantly, not a small part of this amount is going to research centers and universities, which more and more often adapt research and teaching programs to AI-related problems. As an example, it is worth pointing to the Massachusetts Institute of Technology (MIT), which opened a new computer school in 2019 at the expense of USD 1 billion (MIT Stephen A. Schwarzman College of Computing[26]) combining knowledge in the areas of AI, machine learning and data science with other academic disciplines. Due to such a solution, it should be expected that in the nearest future a lot of new, theoretical concepts of practical AI applications will be developed at MIT, with some of them probably being implemented quite soon.

Although artificial intelligence has already completely changed many areas of our daily life, it is difficult to forecast what its development will look like in the coming years or decades. Some scholars believe that we will certainly witness significantly improved quality and performance, for example in areas related to **automatic speech recognition and its conversion to written text, text translation to different languages or texts-to-speech conversion.**[27] In addition, it is expected that artificial intelligence will also make major progress in **identifying faces and images**, especially as for some time a trend has strengthened, related to the improvement in algorithms in this area, with them being already able to obtain information from pixels and "understand" what a particular object should look like. In this context, it should therefore be expected that AI will also provide us with assistance in monitoring and supervising various types of objects, resulting in a reduced workload presently involving humans. Increasingly often scientists and entrepreneurs also expect that in the future, AI will allow robots and **autonomous vehicles** to perform increasingly complicated tasks and they will be adaptable to more and more difficult and dangerous jobs, e.g. in mining (**unmanned coal-cutters**[28]). Furthermore, everyone believes that AI will ensure that safety on the road will gain new, previously unknown, meaning, as artificial intelligence solutions will contribute to its improvement by monitoring vehicle interiors using, e.g. 2D, 3D cameras and sensors, which will be able to check whether the driver is looking at the road, is physically and emotionally "present", is not becoming sleepy, is sober (same for any passengers) and whether he or she is using their phone. These and other innovations are to eliminate the most common cause of accidents, which across the world is human error (in 90 percent of cases), and due to which almost 1.2 million people die on the roads each year. In this context, marketing language aside, the announcements from Volvo engineers sound extremely optimistic, as they are sure that, with modern safety systems as well as their autopilot, no one will die in a vehicle of this brand as from 2020. Interestingly, the company is also willing to pay for any damages that will be caused in the future by their cars.

Artificial intelligence will also lead to unprecedented changes in the field of health services and medicine in general. With in-depth data analysis and machine learning, doctors will gain a new weapon in the fight against the worst diseases and their decisions concerning the selection of medications for patients or the assessment of their health condition will be faster, more accurate and highly personalized. It should be mentioned that people, from the point of view of biology, are very diverse, in terms of genetics, physiognomy, physiology or way of life, while contemporary therapy methods still only account to a limited extent for these differences. Meanwhile, with analyses of large amounts of data that will be supported by computers with high computational powers (High Performance Computing, HPC), it will be possible to better and better **adapt the therapy to the individual genes** of a given patient. In consequence, the treatment will be significantly more purposeful and effective. This will certainly allow doctors (but also medical personnel in general) to gain additional self-confidence at work, in particular in difficult and extreme situations, and create greater trust among patients. AI solutions that will combine elements of software, IT infrastructure (hardware) and wetware systems will also enable, **earlier** than presently, **detection of diseases based not only on laboratory tests, but above all on non-laboratory ones**. In practice, this means that the identification of a disease or illness a patient suffers from will change its present, centuries-old paradigm from "recognition at the patient's bed" to "recognition at the patient's computer". At the same time, clinical diagnosis will gain a new highly personalized dimension just like all of medicine. People with disabilities will be able to expect much greater support on the part of AI. Deaf persons will have the possibility of easier access to science and universities, as developed applications will allow for **lecturers' speech processing into text displayed on the board** in real time. In the case of blind people, artificial intelligence applications, utilizing a camera and sensors, will easily use voice to inform them about objects that are in their way or are within their range of "vision".[29] AI support may also be beneficial for persons suffering from Parkinson's disease who already today can freely use solutions offered by the Industry of the Future, e.g. Liftware, a company created by a group of US scientists and engineers, that offers for sale a device which detects trembling of human hands and differentiates it from these human movements that are made purposefully. In reality this is **smart cutlery** that dampens the user's unwanted movements and thus prevents liquids from spilling or food from being thrown around.[30] The future of the world of medicine is thus very bright, and is due to the fact that every year the health care world invests almost USD 2 billion in AI, and this market, as estimated by experts, will reach the value of USD 17 billion[31] by 2024. In addition, great expectations are vested in hybrid AI applications, which will support clinical doctors in planning therapies, medical examinations, diagnoses and identification of risks. However, it is the doctor who still will be ultimately responsible for care over the patient.

AI will revolutionize not only the world of medicine, science but also education, to the extent that future school or university students will be subjected to precise measurements of personal sensitivity, learning speed or talent identification. Moreover, their written works will be checked and evaluated by devices equipped with AI elements. In practice, any spelling, grammar, punctuation, and styling errors in a text will be verified and evaluated by a dedicated application. In addition, the program will grade each student and suggest possible improvements to the text both in terms of style and content. Alongside the already digital textbooks (e-books), the world of education will also feature virtual teachers as an alternative to traditional education methods. It is also expected that "machine-teachers" will solve the problems faced by contemporary schools, challenged by, among other issues, overcrowded classes, overworked teachers or the level of education. Important changes in the context of AI further development are also expected in the financial services sector which, as no other one, is exposed to frequent systems breakdowns and cybernetic attacks. AI tools that are to emerge on this market in the near future will not only warn bank authorities against system malfunctions and the dangers of malicious attacks, but also better identify persons who are responsible for them. As in the case of **virtual teachers** in schools, virtual advisors are to appear in financial institutions. This solution does not come as a surprise, especially since currently many banks already utilize the idea of **robo-advisory**, namely financial and/or investment consulting with minimal human involvement. However, it should be mentioned that the constantly growing AI abilities allow the analysis of constantly growing amounts of data, which is particularly important for the financial sector, verifying hundreds of information packages every day, perhaps in order to make the right credit decision for the client. It also seems to be a matter of time before credit decisions will finally be made by robots. Robots will also perform functions of **virtual assistants** in customer service departments as in the future almost every company, regardless of the sector, having such a department will aim, if not to exclude humans completely from this process, then to restrict human involvement to the necessary minimum. Virtual assistants will thus gradually replace people employed in such departments, and soon their intelligence will allow them to call us to arrange a meeting. If for any reason the date and time of the meeting are inconvenient for us, the assistant "will understand this" and propose another date. Next to virtual assistants, frequent relations with customers will be sustained by the technology of intuitive chat bots. In practice, these are applications containing the interlocutor (a window with the consultant's photograph "popping up" at the corner of the screen), who will always be ready to help us. In the future, due to the use of hybrid AI solutions, this technology will be even more advanced, allowing chat bots to better perform any assigned business tasks, make better decisions related to planning flights, booking hotels or shopping. Furthermore, this technology will gain "new features", meaning a transition from the currently used graphical user interfaces[32] (GUI), to conversational user interfaces (CUI), which resemble a natural conversation with a "living" person. It is expected that CUI technology will be a key trend for several decades, and chat bots will create an exceptional subsector for the global personal consulting industry.

Apart from an improvement in maintaining close customer relations, AI, including predictive algorithms and machine learning, will **enhance the quality**, and hence **the accuracy of any present predictions and forecasts**. From the point of view of industry these tools will be particularly useful for production departments, where effective delivery and optimization of inventory are critical for profitability and income from the operations performed (Shabbir & Anwer, 2015). However, from the point of view of the judiciary, the use of AI raises immense controversies or even objections of persons operating in this domain. The main focus here is on using them both to predict rulings that will be issued by a particular judge and to determine the duration of a custodial sentence. In the former case, predictive analysis is to be based on an examination of any rulings issued in the past, and in the latter one on the suspect's history. In this context, the possibility is being posited that predictive algorithms may ignore or favor specific data, for example pertaining to the affective spheres of human life (feelings, mental conditions). Bearing in mind these and other controversies, the development of artificial intelligence, in particular in this ethical and moral aspect, is increasingly becoming a topic of detailed discussions among both ethicists and philosophers as well as governments. New concepts in general, and new technologies in particular, have always posed and will continue to pose a real threat that their commercial use will be to the detriment of the future and human rights. In the case of artificial intelligence, where we are dealing with generating, collecting, processing and sharing growing amounts of data on a daily basis (both in individual and collective terms) the problem seems to be at least twice as difficult. In fact, on the one hand, the scale of collected information gives us huge abilities in profiling and predicting future human behaviors, but, on the other hand, it may expose us to the loss of privacy, the right to free speech or information. Therefore, not only those

Table 2.5 Prospects of AI application in various sectors of the economy

Area	*AI-based solutions – possible applications*
Power industry	Management and optimization of processes related to power grid load. Preventive maintenance of power units. Improvement of power unit control systems. Identification of illegal energy collection.
Agriculture	Prediction of yields based on the analysis of satellite images. Crop structure management. Selective spraying of individual plants instead of whole fields. Prevention of crop diseases. Autonomous agricultural machines. Sowing schedule management.
Logistics	Optimization of vehicle loading and routes. Optimization of intermodal traffic. Autonomous and semi-autonomous trucks. E-commerce delivery robots. Optimization of railway route load. Optimization of technical pause and train repair planning. Prediction of delays in transport. Optimization and dynamic change of railway travel schedules. Optimization of traffic control in cities. Storehouse management with the help of robots.
Industry	Plant building optimization. Optimization of production process control. Reduction of waste generated in production. Increased effectiveness of industrial plants. Reduction of supply chain errors (reduced costs concerning e.g. manufacturing, storage, packing, transport and supply chain). Design of machines. Identification of the reasons for failures of machines and necessary design changes.
Sales and Marketing	Customer and customer need positioning. Product design to suit customer needs. Building optimal marketing messages. Detecting customer emotions. Selecting products to suit customer taste or needs. Automatic creation of product descriptions. Automation in running marketing campaigns. Construction and design of empathic advertisements. Recommendation systems dedicated to e-commerce platforms. Smart mirrors and changing rooms.
State administration	Detecting tax fraud. Sealing of the tax system. Offices' new contact channels with citizens and interactive citizen services. Detecting payment fraud. Detecting document forgeries. Optimization of responding to crisis situations. Assignment of incoming documentation. Detecting unauthorized access in electronic systems. Detecting "hazardous" provisions in local administration agreements.

(*Continued*)

Table 2.5 (*Continued*)

Area	*AI-based solutions – possible applications*
Cybersecurity	Identification of ongoing attacks. Profiling network applications and users in order to detect anomalies. Identification of attacks and gaps in systems. Identification of network attack scenarios. Monitoring of networks and applications.

Source: Study based on data from Polish Ministry of Digitization (2018).

described above, but all other modern AI-based solutions (see Table 2.5) must be implemented in a responsible manner in the future, taking account of, on the one hand, the needs and expectations, but, on the other hand, possible hazards and dangers for all stakeholders.

To conclude, we should mention that for most economic sectors the prospects for the application of AI-based solutions are very promising (see Table 2.5). However, a lot of them are just at the start of this process. Notwithstanding the above, the industrial revolution happening before our eyes is a fact and there is no possibility to stop it. At the same time, the world will be subject to further, intensive changes and so will AI. It can be concluded with a great deal of probability that **its present model** based to a large extent on **computer software and infrastructure** (software–hardware) will evolve **towards** a **model** based on **computer software, infrastructure and biological systems** (software–hardware–wetware). In the future this gradual transformation will allow AI to increasingly imitate the operations of the human brain, the more so because the development of AI from the model software–hardware–wetware will probably evolve further, towards the software–hardware–chemware model[33] (see Figure 2.4).

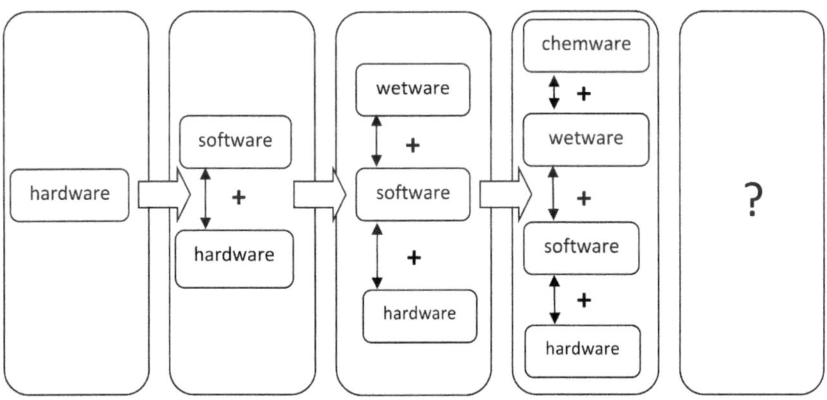

Figure 2.4 Staged development model of AI systems. Source: Authors' own study.

Notes

1 John McCarthy was born in Boston in 1927 and died in 2011, in Stanford. He was a professor at the universities in Princeton, Stanford and Dartmouth. In 1971, for his contribution to the development of the artificial intelligence domain he was awarded the Turing Award (annual prize given by the Association for Computing Machinery – ACM – for outstanding achievements in information technology). On the other hand, in 1988 he won the Kyoto Prize (funded by Japanese billionaire, philanthropist and Buddhist monk Dr. Kazuo Inamori) in advanced technologies.
2 Heuristic methods are one of the most important artificial intelligence tools.
3 Richard Bellman died at age of 64 in New York in 1984. In 1979 he received an honorary medal given by the Institute of Electrical and Electronics Engineers (IEEE) for his contribution to the development of the decision-making process control theory, including for the development of problem areas related to dynamic programming.
4 Algorithmics is a domain of computer technology and cybernetics focused on the science of algorithms.
5 As an example, at this point it is worth mentioning the 2019 takeover, by technological giant Alibaba for USD 103 million, of Berlin startup Data Artisans, which provided distributed systems and large-scale data streaming services for enterprises. Data Artisans, it should be emphasized, was founded only five years earlier, in 2014.
6 Also known as Light AI (LAI).
7 Also known as Full AI (FAI).
8 Meanwhile, in the book "Alone Together" published in 2011 by Sherry Turkle we can read that: simulated thinking can be thinking, but a simulated feeling is not a feeling. Simulated love is not love.
9 American computer scientist, University of Stanford professor-emeritus in computer science, regarded as the "father of expert systems". In 1994 he won the Alan Turing Award (see note [1] in this chapter).
10 In 1965, in *Information and Control* he published an article on fuzzy sets and logic entitled: "Fuzzy Sets".
11 This notion originates from the field of mathematical optimization. Gradient optimization methods are techniques utilizing numerical algorithms, and thus ways of solving mathematical problems with the use of operations on numbers, in search for the minima of the preset functions of the objective.
12 A breakthrough in this area was made in 1986 as a result of publishing the article, authored by Rumelhart, Hinton and Williams, entitled: "Learning representations by back-propagating errors".
13 Read more at: https://futureoflife.org.
14 Apollo Guidance Computer, AGC. It weighed 32 kg (sic!).
15 Currently, companies that, starting from the beginning of their operations, aim at globalization and quick internationalization, without the preceding period of gradual internationalization, are called "born global companies". Two types can be distinguished in the professional literature, namely: export/import start up and global startup companies.
16 PricewaterhouseCoopers.
17 S-CGE model (Spatial Computable General Equilibrium), namely a model of spatial evaluation of the general equilibrium is a dynamic model of the global economy that was developed by the experts from PwC, to evaluate the global (net) effect of AI on the global economy by 2030. From the technical point of view it models economic interactions among various entities present in the economy, while "general equilibrium" in the model means that it represents a closed system, which treats the flow of resources from one field (or from one player) to another as a closed circuit. Importantly, this model takes account of a number of intricacies, including e.g. expectations of households, present in the realities of the business world.

18 Network effect is a situation where the "values" for the consumer evolve with the number of users of the given product or service.
19 For more information, see Chapter 2.2.
20 For more information, see Chapter 1.1.
21 "S" curve is a graphic presentation of the development trends that systems, things, products, services, etc. are subject to. "S" curve consists of five stages including: stage 1 – garage enthusiasts, stage 2 – mass popularity, stage 3 – development slowdown, stage 4 – market death, stage 5 – second life (though this stage is extremely rare in practice).
22 For more information, see Chapter 2.2.
23 Nearly 200 million persons all over the world use the application of and visit Amazon .com each month.
24 www.zhihu.com.
25 Thus, the "connected intelligence" concept.
26 The name of the school bears the name of Stephen A. Schwarzman, co-founder and director general of *Blackstone* fund, which supported the creation of a new computer school within MIT with the amount of USD 350 million. For more information, see: https://computing.mit.edu/.
27 Already today some translators can translate a million words in only one second.
28 In Poland such vehicles are already used e.g. in copper mines operated by KGHM Polska Miedź S.A.
29 As an example, it is worth mentioning an artificial intelligence-based application developed by Microsoft called Seeing AI.
30 According to the company's data Liftware "smart cutlery" is shaking 70 percent less than the hand of a sick person.
31 For more information, see the report: *Artificial Intelligence in Medicine Market – Growth, Trends, and Forecast (2019–2024).*
32 At present, hundreds of millions of people worldwide already interact with personal digital assistants on such platforms as Google, Apple or Amazon.
33 Chemical systems.

References

Accenture. (2018). A technology revolution like no other. In *Explained a Guide for Executives*. Accenture Applied Intelligence. Accenture Global.

AiLab. (2019). *AiLab Artificial Intelligence Glossary*. Downloaded 12 September 2019 from: https://www.ailab.com.au/resources/ai-glossary/.

Bellman, R. (1978). *An Introduction to Artificial Intelligence: Can Computers Think?* San Francisco: Boyd & Fraser Publishing Company.

Boucher, P. (2019). *How Artificial Intelligence Works*. European Parliamentary Research Service. Scientific Foresight Unit (STOA). Panel for the Future of Science and Technology.

Bowser, A., Sloan, M., Michelucci, P., & Pauwels, E. (2017). *Artificial Intelligence: A Policy-Oriented Introduction*. Washington, DC: The Wilson Center.

Ernst, E., Merola, R., & Samaan, D. (2018). *The Economics of Artificial Intelligence: Implications for the Future of Work*. ILO Future of Work Research Paper Series. Geneva, Switzerland: International Labour Office.

Etzioni, O. (2016). *No, the Experts Don't Think Superintelligent AI is a Threat to Humanity*. MIT Technology Review. Downloaded 12 September 2019 from: https://www.technologyreview.com/s/602410/no-the-experts-dont-think-superintelligent-aiis-a-threat-tohumanity/.

Gillham, J., Rimmington, L., Dance, H., Verweij, G., Rao, A., Roberts, K. B., & Paich, M. (2018). *The Macroeconomic Impact of Artificial Intelligence*. London: PwC.

Latentview. (2018). How to make artificial intelligence work for your organization. *Business Analytics*. Downloaded 4 September 2019 from: https://www.latentview.com/blog/business-benefit-from-ai/.

Li, W., Wu, W. J., Wang, H. M., Cheng, X. J., Chen, H. J., Zhou, Z. H., & Ding, R. (2017). Crowd intelligence in AI 2.0 era. *Front. Inform. Technol. Electron. Eng.*, 18(1), pp. 15–43. DOI: org/10.1631/FITEE.1601859.

Manyika, J., & Bughin, J. (2018). *The Promise and Challenge of the Age of Artificial Intelligence*. McKinsey Global Institute: New York.

Nazri, A., Azim Abd Ghani, A., Hafez, I., & Ng, K. Y. (2018). A new theoretical framework for testing consciousness in a machine. In International Conference on Soft Computing and Data Mining (SCDM, 2018). Recent Advances on Soft Computing and Data Mining, pp. 330–339. Malaysia. Johor.

Organisation for Economic Co-operation and Development. (2016). *OECD Science, Technology and Innovation Outlook 2016*. Paris: OECD Publishing. Downloaded from: https://www.ewivlaanderen.be/sites/default/files/bestanden/oecd_science_technology_and_innovation_outlook_2016.pdf.

Pan, Y. (2016). Heading toward artificial intelligence 2.0. *Engineering*, *2*, pp. 409–413.

Pan, Y. (2017). Special issue on Artificial intelligence 2.0. *Front. Inf. Technol. Electron. Eng.*, *18*(1), pp. 1–2. DOI: 10.1631/FITEE.1710000.

Paschek, D., Luminosu, C. T., & Draghici, A. (2017). Automated business process management: In times of digital transformation using machine learning or artificial intelligence. In MATEC Web of Conferences, Sibiu, Romania. DOI: 10.1051/matecconf/20171210.

Pei, J., Deng, L., Song, S., Zhao, M., Zhang, Y., Wu, S., Wang, G., Zou, Z., Wu, Z., Wei, H., Chen, F., Deng, N., Wu, S., Wang, Y., Wu, Y., Yang, Z., Ma, Ch., Li, G., Han, W., Li, H., Wu, H., Zhao, R., Xie, Y., & Shi, L. (2019). Towards artificial general intelligence with hybrid Tianjic chip architecture. *Nature*, *572*, pp. 106–111.

Perez, J. A., Deligianni, F., Ravi, D., & Yang G. Z. (2017). *Artificial Intelligence and Robotics*. UK-RAS White Papers. London: UK-RAS Network Robotics and Autonomous Systems.

Polish Ministry of Digitization (2018). *Assumptions for the AI strategy in Poland*. Warsaw, Poland: Polish Ministry of Digitization.

Purdy, M., & Daugherty, P. (2016). *Why Artificial Intelligence is the Future of Growth*. Accenture Global: Dublin.

Revell, T. (2017). AI will be able to beat us at everything by 2060, say expert. *New Scientist*. Downloaded 12 September 2019 from: https://www.newscientist.com/article/2133188-ai-will-be-able-to-beat-us-at-everything-by-2060-say-experts/.

Saxena, A., & Gopal, K. S. (2013). Quantum artificial consciousness. In Conference: Emerging Trends in Computer Science Research and Developement (ETCRD), Haridwar, Volume: Special Volume.

Shabbir, J., & Anwer, T. (2015). Artificial intelligence and its role in near future. *J. Latex Class Files*, *14*(8), pp. 1–11.

Siljebrít, H., Addyman, C., & Pickering, A. (2018). Towards human-like artificial intelligence using StarCraft 2. In Foundations of Digital Games 2018 (FDG18), August 7–10, 2018, Malmö, Sweden. New York: ACM. DOI: org/10.1145/3235765.3235811.

Szczepański, M. (2019). *Economic Impacts of Artificial Intelligence (AI)*. Brussels: European Parliamentary Research Service, EPRS. European Parliament.

Tian, Y. H., Chen, X. L., Xiong, H. K., Li, H. L., Dai, L. R., Chen, J., Xing, J. L., Chen, J., Wu, X. H., Hu, W. M., Hu, Y., Huang, T. J., & Gao, W. (2017). Towards human-like and transhuman perception in AI 2.0: A review. *Front. Inform. Technol. Electron. Eng.*, *18*(1), pp. 58–67.

United Nations Conference on Trade and Development. (2017). *Digitalization, Trade and Development*. Information Economy Report 2017. Geneva: UNCTAD. Downloaded 1 December 2019 from: https://unctad.org/en/PublicationsLibrary/ier2017_en./ier2017_en.pdf.

Xue, J. R., Wang, D., Du, S. Y., Cui, D. X., Huang, Y., & Zheng, N. N. (2017). A vision-centered multi-sensor fusing approach to self-localization and obstacle perception for robotic cars. *Front. Inform. Technol. Electron. Eng.*, *18*(1), pp. 122–138. DOI: org/10.1631/FITEE.1601873.

Zhang, T., Li, Q., Zhang, C. S., Liang, H. W., Li, P., Wang, T. M., Shuo, L., Zhu, Y. L., & Cheng, W. (2017). Current trends in the development of intelligent unmanned autonomous systems. *Front. Inform. Technol. Electron. Eng.*, *18*(1), pp. 68–85. DOI: org/10.1631/FITEE.1601650.

Zhou, L. K., Tang, S. L., Xiao, J., Wu, F., & Zhuang, Y. T. (2017). Disambiguating named entities with deep supervised learning via crowd labels. *Front. Inform. Technol. Electron. Eng.*, *18*(1), pp. 97–106. DOI: org/10.1631/FITEE.1601835.

Zhuang, Y. T., Wu, F., Chen, C., & Pan, Y. H. (2017). Challenges and opportunities: From big data to knowledge in AI 2.0. *Front. Inform. Technol. Electron. Eng.*, *18*(1), pp. 3–14. DOI: org/10.1631/FITEE.1601883.

3 Organizations in the artificial intelligence era

3.1 Impact of artificial intelligence on the organization

Technological changes, shaped above all by the rapid development of new IT technologies, the final effect of which is creation of innovative products and services, are the most important external factors causing changes in organizations. Their impact is often large enough to change not only the organizations themselves, but also the mechanisms of the world economy. An example of such influence of technology on the organization and its environment, both the close (task-oriented), and further one (macro-environment), was the Internet, which has made major (often irreversible) changes in the everyday functioning of both the world and its component parts. At present, many experts and scholars believe that the same will apply to the concept of artificial intelligence development which is expected to change humanity over the next two decades more than it changed over the last three centuries. However, the nature of the changes, including their power and scope of influence, will finally be dependent on, among other things, the readiness that the organizations and their management boards will demonstrate when it comes to utilizing AI potential. State authorities will also have a role to play in this area, as they should ultimately supervise and control the ways of using and utilizing AI systems and systems used by programmers employed in organizations. Artificial intelligence, including its potential and power to impact the environment, is characterized by the fact that, with no control, it can create adverse effects for the organization in general, and its stakeholders in particular. Some time ago, Elon Musk[1] also expressed his concerns in this regard during a conversation on CNBC, stating that: "artificial intelligence is more dangerous than nuclear weapons". He added that in the future its omnipresence may become extremely burdensome for humans. However, regardless of how experts, scientists, businesspeople, visionaries and other stakeholders perceive the development of AI worldwide, it is undeniable is that at present it plays a leading role in changing the world and mankind, especially because of significant achievements in AI still seem to be ahead of us. Such a conclusion can be drawn at least from the analysis of organizations' global expenses on AI systems (see Figure 3.1), which, as indicated by forecasts, by 2023 may reach a level close to USD 100 billion worldwide. In practice, this means that in just two years the

DOI: 10.4324/9781003184027-3

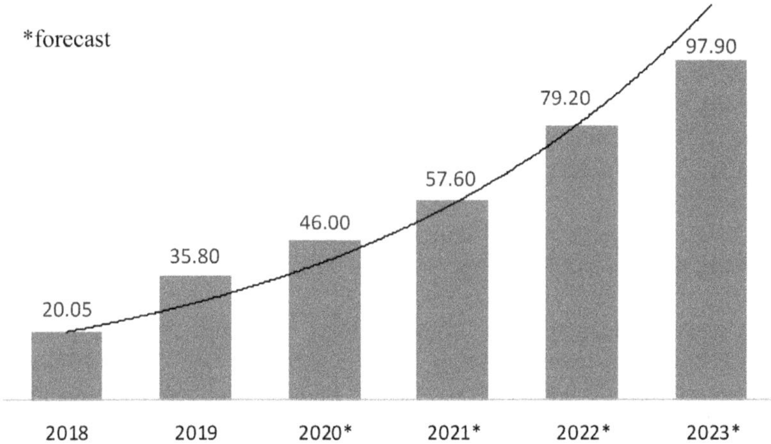

Figure 3.1 Expenditures by global organizations on AI systems (USD billion). Note: *forecast. Source: Prepared by the authors based on e.g. (IDC) Worldwide Artificial Intelligence Spending Guide.

amount that organizations will invest in AI-based solutions will increase almost four times and will amount to approximately USD 80 billion. There are several reasons why investment in AI is continuously popular. First, organizations perceive the AI concept as humanity's contemporary invention that is worth investing in. Second, they want to stay competitive, especially as compared to those companies from their sector that already apply AI-based solutions. Third, they hope for increased incomes. Fourth, the adaptation of AI in most areas of their operations is to ensure greater effectiveness, primarily as a result of savings and improvements in the company. Fifth, persons who manage organizations are convinced that, with AI, their information and data will allow them to better plan and forecast needs of their customers.

Sixth, we see a conviction that AI will increase the efficiency of the organization's business or manufacturing processes. And seventh, organizations believe that AI technology will become a significant source of value for them. However, bearing in mind the above, it turns out that for most organizations, investment in AI-based solutions are a prerequisite but an insufficient one to be successful thanks to the application of this technology. As confirmed by global research conducted in 2019 by MIT Sloan Management Review and Boston Consulting Group (BCG)[2] organizations must additionally possess a characteristic set of organizational behaviors, in order to take advantage of the value offered by AI (Ransbotham et al., 2019). The following behaviors are indicated:

- ability to combine (integrate) AI strategies with the organization's general business strategy,

- active undertaking of, often risky, efforts for AI, where the priority will be income growth and not expense reduction,
- efficient AI adjustment to the level of required production and expected consumption, by creating proper business models and correctly functioning processes,
- consolidation of initiatives in AI with broader efforts for a business transformation which can prove necessary in order to maintain competitive advantage,
- additional investment in process improvement, the quality of collected and processed data, knowledge about AI and in AI talent in the organization.

All of the above "unconventional" organizational behaviors of enterprises, in combination with investment in AI, are to help them increase the benefits and opportunities offered by AI technology, while limiting problems in generating value using AI. The same research (Ransbotham et al., 2019), argues that organizations that concentrate solely on AI production, including on creation of tools, generation of data, or development of technologies, have smaller chances to gain value from AI than companies that actively integrate the organization's owners, processes or AI users. In practice, differentiation of these two approaches of organizations to AI technology is significant in that ultimately they will determine the final success – or failure – of a particular company, especially since the true success of organizations in the world of AI will depend both on generating revenue as well as skillful reinvestment of funds to deepen its ability to utilize AI across the whole enterprise.

Surprisingly, the present artificial intelligence wave is more a **revolution in data analysis** than a **revolution resulting from new technological tools**, as it is data along with algorithms that form the two crucial artificial intelligence elements. When it comes to algorithms, essentially being a description of methods of conduct leading to a particular result, they were invented a long time ago – the first references about them date back to the times of Euclid, the ancient Greek mathematician. In the case of data, the situation is different; the world has never before experienced such a level of their aggregation. In other words, large amounts of data coming from various sources are aggregated into one whole (data composition). This new phenomenon, popularizing the availability of large amounts of data in a simple form, raises first of all the interest of organizations that perceive data at present as the most valuable resource within their structures. At present, data inflow into the organization comes from any possible source, including operating systems, transaction systems, platforms and websites, scanners, sensors, loudspeakers, smart sensors, satellites, CPS systems, images or social media. In this context, it can be proposed that in the nearest future what will distinguish some organizations will be data and the ability to manage them, namely: obtain, store, organize and process. This statement is also supported by new trends in the global economy, visible for some time, concerning change in the present knowledge-based economy paradigm towards the data-driven economy paradigm and the evolution of big data also towards fast data collections.

Since a successful digital transformation, increasingly defined by social sciences as a civilization megatrend of our times, is not possible without data and artificial intelligence, it will be impossible for organizations that will only collect data and not skillfully process them to achieve competitive advantage in the digital economy. In fact, in the digital economy, what matters is not the ability of a particular entity to accumulate information (data), but how it will be, first of all, processed and, secondly, utilized. This, however, involves the need to redefine and follow the vision of the company in the world based on artificial intelligence, algorithms and robots. In practice, a well-defined vision of the organization will serve in these conditions to build a strong strategy based on data as its key resource. For an organization's data-based strategy to succeed, it is necessary to:

- make the selection of data (data quality),
- prepare and implement procedures determining the ways of general data utilization in the organization,
- prepare and implement procedures determining the ways of utilizing the organization's internal data for its internal and external use,
- prepare and implement procedures determining the ways of utilizing the organization's external data for its internal and external use,
- develop a new shape of the business model that will take account of the specific nature of the organization and its products, from the point of view of the adopted strategy and financial results,
- prepare and implement procedures determining access to data,
- prepare and implement procedures determining the ways of data management,
- conduct research on the opportunities to develop and use large data collections,
- participate in data ecosystems on the local and global level.

In the context of the presented elements forming the process of building an organization's data-based strategy, special attention must be paid to the one concerning their participation in **data ecosystems**. In the artificial intelligence era they are defined as relational networks of entities which directly and indirectly consume, produce or deliver data and other related resources (Schatsky et al., 2019). The organization's participation in **partner ecosystems** is an additional value that they can derive from the AI world. In fact the platform technology will foster an increase in their competences in many areas, including analyses of product management, business market and competitors, sector attractiveness, business model, data and the organization's abilities to use them, legal issues or identification of risks and risk management methods. In addition, as part of creating these **multi-entity organizational structures**, organizations will quickly identify data, both internal and external, that will be valuable for them and adapted to their business strategies (Schatsky et al., 2019). In this context, it may be presumed that organizations which do not build their strategies on data in the AI era, or where data are not a significant element in it, will be pushed out to the margin of the new, digital reality.

In connection with the above, it is easy to observe that data-driven artificial intelligence not only changes the organizational diagrams of organizations themselves or their key resources, but also determines their development strategies and redefines their strategic alliances. The pace of these changes often results from the size of the organization. In fact large organizations demonstrate a proportionally greater commitment to the adaptation of AI-based solutions than small organizations, chiefly because they naturally have easier access to much greater data resources (at least internal ones) than smaller organizations. Does this mean that small organizations are at a disadvantage compared to large ones, especially when it comes to adaptation abilities and deriving the benefits offered by AI? The answer to this question is no. Small organizations are not powerless here, and "small" does not mean "capable of less". Considering the adaptation processes in AI, for some time small organizations have already been characterized by:

- better organization of work in the context of adaptation of AI-based solutions,
- better data management level,
- growing participation in business ecosystems,
- better identification of market needs in the AI area.

This means that, with gradually decreasing artificial intelligence infrastructure costs, their bargaining power in relation to large organizations will continue to grow. However, the AI utilization level in the organization and the related benefits being derived will ultimately not be determined by either its size or the amount of data possessed, but by the organization's adaptation capabilities. In practice, this will come down to the scale of effective implementation and daily use of AI tools in particular areas of the organization. The efficiency of operating the whole set of AI instruments in the organization will depend on the creative utilization of data by its AI leaders.

In the end, it is impossible not to agree with the argument that artificial intelligence, whose analyses or assessments are faster, more efficient or more relevant than those formulated by humans, and bear a significantly lower error rate, is a powerful tool both for individual entities as well as organizations. If applied properly, it can be a blessing for people and increase the organizations' business efficiency as well as strengthening partnerships. In the case of organizations, a significant majority of which are still in the initial phase of the AI era-related transformation, their final structure and profile of operation still remain unclear. At the same time, they need more time for their business model to be adjusted to the needs of the organization, the environment of which is at present simultaneously postmodern and turbulent. However, from the point of view of the future and the changes taking place, four areas will be of crucial importance in the process of transforming today's organizations into organizations operating within the AI environment (AI organizations), namely (*The Economist*, 2019):

- area I: data resources in the organization. The organization's strategy will be based on data as a key resource. In addition, organizations will aim to

maximize their abilities in processes related to the processing and use of information (both internal and external),
- area II: size of the organization. AI technology will not favor any particular size of the organization. However, small organizations will change their structures under the influence of the benefits derived from cooperation with the AI environment. Furthermore, small organizations will, to a growing extent, rely on outsourcing and partnerships for delivery of non-core activities,
- area III: human resources in the organization. AI leaders will set the tone for the organizations operating in the AI world. Workers, in terms of access to data and analyses, will have almost the same abilities that are awarded in this regard to senior personnel,
- area IV: ethics in the organization. New legal and administrative regulations will ensure that the ethics of AI implementation in different areas of the organization will become a frequent subject of the management staff's meetings.

These changes will require time from organizations. However, it should be expected that they will happen faster rather than slower, in particular in the environment of those organizations whose managerial staff already have clearly specified goals for its future: a future which will be marked by the data-based digital economy. And even though the related AI technology will not replace humans, it will require organizations to train them. It is estimated that by 2021 it will be necessary to train almost 120 million employees in the 12 largest economies of the world (Aon, 2019). This means that AI will strongly interfere with their present work and skills. It may quickly turn out that inborn intelligence (Intelligence Quotient, IQ) and emotional intelligence (Emotional Quotient, EQ) will be prerequisite but still insufficient conditions for an employee to be successful in an AI-based organization. In fact, these two abilities will have to be supplemented with another one, related to digital intelligence (Digital Quotient, DQ). Generally, it can be presumed that success in life will soon depend not only on one's intellect and emotion management skills, but also, and perhaps first of all, on cognitive skills, which help face any challenges and adjust to the requirements of digital life. Formulation of new strategic and operating plans in the organization as well as management of its key resources will therefore require from the managers both great responsibility as well as supervision in all the business areas covered by AI.

3.2 Artificial intelligence – changing managerial paradigms

Convictions, imaginations, theories and assumptions have a considerable effect on how we operate, not only as individuals, but also as a community. A collection of all elements that determine our way of seeing the world is what defines the term **paradigm**. The author of the theory of paradigms, American science philosopher Thomas Kuhn, in his book *The Structure of Scientific Revolutions*,[3] defined them as patterns that are the solution to a certain problem, accepted by the scientific community. In addition, he emphasized that science does not develop as a linear accumulation of new knowledge but is subject to periodic revolutions referred to as paradigm changes. This means that we can formulate an opinion that the development of science is equal to the sum of its paradigm changes. However, it should be noticed that a paradigm change, both in life as well as in science, is not easy or frequent. Often many years must elapse, and sometimes even centuries, as in the case of the heliocentric theory of the world, before an evolution occurs in the current way of thinking about life, the world or science. A similar situation is the case for some paradigms in management sciences, unchanged since the times of Henry Fayol or Frederick Taylor. However, in recent years, a substantial number of them have evolved, mainly due to the challenges that the economic environment created for organizations, managers and employees. At present, the situation is repeated. In order to face it anew, another change in thinking about management is necessary, as it is impossible to tackle contemporary management problems with the use of old methods, techniques or tools. The development of Industry 4.0, driven by AI technology, in fact redefines both the nature and the general principles of management. Transformations encompass whole sectors, industries, organizations, societies or existing business models. In response to such turbulent changes in the general environment of organizations, especially the technological one (see Table 3.1), the present patterns of management must also be subject to evolution. In practice, this applies to their adaptation to the postmodern (post-traditional) model of the socio-economic reality, in which order and linearity have been pushed out by coincidence, decomposition and impermanence of phenomena.

Table 3.1 Technologies that will change the present paradigm in management of an organization

In your opinion, which technology area will change the "life" of the organization?	
Technology	*Percentage of answers of the management staff (n = 2835)*
Artificial intelligence/machine learning	89%
Data analysis (including predictive analysis)	69%
Computing cloud (including XaaS services)	36%
Internet of Things	27%
Digital transformation	26%
5G technology	18%
Blockchain technology	14%
Automation	13%
Specialist software	11%
Business analysis	10%
Business process robotization	9%
ERP	7%
CRM	6%
Digitalization	6%
Immersive experience technology	5%
Cybersecurity	4%
Web and online technologies (APIs)	3%

Source: Authors' own study on the basis of Kelner and Kostadinov (2019).

Bearing in mind the inevitability of change, questions arise considering what transformations will apply to the present shape of management, including its paradigms (see Table 3.2), in the artificial intelligence era? Will the present models functioning in the organization, related to leadership, motivation, communication or work organization be largely transformed? Furthermore, what will be their scale and effect on organizations? Answering such questions is not easy, mostly due to the complexity of the topic discussed and the prediction process itself, which by its nature bears certain errors. However, a literature review on this topic permits a few key areas to be identified, where the present management practices (paradigms) will be replaced by new ones (see Table 3.2). They will relate to: administration, organization and ways of performing work by the management staff, employee motivation systems, leadership and operations (see Kolbjørnsrud et al., 2016a).

In the case of administrative activities, it is undisputable that many of them will be automated by AI, as these are often not very complex and routine tasks, and thus easily subject to the digitization process, particularly as, according to research performed by Accenture on a group of almost 1800 managers, they spend most of their work time (54 percent) on administrative tasks. In consequence, only 30 percent is left for solving problems faced daily by the organization and only 7 percent for talking with their associates (Kolbjørnsrud et al., 2016b). However, AI solutions will reverse these proportions. Instead managers will gain additional time for the matters that essentially should be a priority in their daily work and which will directly apply to actual management and not only to, as before, e.g. continuous reporting (creating reports). Therefore, their role will evolve more towards soft than hard skills. It should also be expected that in the near future, AI and not managers will be involved in maintaining and controlling work schedules or managing budgets of the company's particular organizational units. This means that the organization's management will gain more time and opportunities to work on more interesting projects, giving better prospects for both the organization and for self-realization.

When it comes to the organization and the way of performing work, it will require a different approach from the managerial staff. The main focus will be put above all on an assessment of the situation by the manager that will take account of his or her previous experience in making important decisions and solving complex problems. Such an approach will also have to consider his or her skills of critical and analytical thinking combined with AI cooperation. Knowledge of organizational history and culture as well as the ability to show empathy and demonstrate ethical judgment of action will be a significant addition to any managerial qualifications possessed. People will be focused on processes and generating ideas, while AI will support them in solving current problems. Teamwork, mostly due to the diversity of cognitive perspectives, will continue to be an important element in work culture in organizations. In addition, building and sustaining relations, or employees' application of networking will be key tools in developing both their abilities and business. Therefore, organizations must take care to create proper conditions that will take account of additional people, tangible, intangible, or time resources, if necessary. In other words, they must adjust the development of new staff skills, adding digital skills, creative thinking, experimenting, data

Table 3.2 Classification of management paradigms – a universal perspective

Paradigm	*Areas*	*Description*
Leadership and control	Action philosophy	A clear separation of cognitive processes from manufacturing processes, namely thinking from action. Due to limited efficiency, the workforce must be strictly controlled in order to obtain the assumed effects and the efficiency level. Mechanistic organization, with strong red tape, with clearly specified work rules and continuous control. Operations related to competitors strongly focused on destroying enemies.
	Leadership	Strong, heroic style of leadership focused on tasks, with the use of the elements of, primarily psychological, coercion. Putting high pressure on human skills and inborn intelligence.
	Motivation	The motivation process includes only safety, economic but also physical motives, mostly triggered by fear and a system of sanctions.
	Communication	The communication process consists in the top-down flow of information, often distorted and treated suspiciously by subordinates.
	Operative model	Strong hierarchy. Positions and titles have importance in the organizational culture.
	Final results	Paradigm frequently applied in extraordinary and crisis situations (military operations). It can be characterized by short-term results in difficult situations. Approach with positive results in the performance of repeatable large-scale processes, well known to the employees. Often used in the 20th-century industrial revolutions.
Anticipation and control	Action philosophy	Stimulating actions in the organization using optimistic forecasts and incentives from its external immediate and further environment. Organization functioning according to system 2 (behavioral model). Control process designed on the basis of hierarchical dependence and top-down determined goals. Scale of competition is treated as an essential measure of short-term success.
	Leadership	Putting strong pressure on inborn intelligence. Utilization of Microsoft Excel as a support tool for management processes in the organization. Task-focused leadership.
	Motivation	Motivation process supported by incentives and promised prizes, with simultaneous existence of sanctions and fear in its toolset.
	Communication	Communication process consists in the top-down information flow (cascade–multi-level communication forms). Low scale of suspiciousness in top-down transmitted information.

(*Continued*)

Table 3.2 (*Continued*)

Paradigm	*Areas*	*Description*
	Operative model	Hierarchical distribution of operating plans in the organization. Greater freedom in action on work posts. Management based on continuous monitoring of key performance indicators. Management model strongly focused on fulfillment of the defined goals. Hazard of losing a job in the case of no effects.
	Final results	Paradigm frequently used in a stable business environment. Evaluated in a long-term perspective. Used in management of a set of several business-wise independent organizations.
High level of autonomy	Action philosophy	Organization's obtained performance is a derivative of its autonomy in both individual and team action. Strength of the organization lies in its independence, transparency of activities and common thinking about its good and success. Organic type of organization, exhibiting great flexibility to the surrounding business environment. Competitors perceived as a positive challenge and an opportunity to be successful in the long term.
	Leadership	Leadership based on inborn intelligence and emotional intelligence, necessary to inspire individuals and manage the mental condition and teams' cooperation in the system. Leaders acting as a "stimulus" for creating value in the organization. Strong leadership, its different styles as a matter of fact, pursued depending on the situation. Relational approach in fulfillment of the set operating plans. Creating a cooperative, trusting and security-oriented work environment.
	Motivation	Motivation process is built by different methods of participation in the organization's operations. Employees have a favorable approach to their managers.
	Communication	Free flow of information in the organization – bottom-up and top-down as well as horizontally. Information characterized by a low degree of distortion.
	Operative model	Creating high transparency and common awareness across the entire organization. High autonomy of particular employees and teams in pursuing the organization's fundamental business objectives. Implementation of the model of partnership as well as cooperation with independent teams and experts. Tasks in the organization often achieved in the matrix-based system. Continuous monitoring, supervision and evaluation of any projects implemented in the organization.

(*Continued*)

Table 3.2 (*Continued*)

Paradigm	*Areas*	*Description*
	Final results	Highly adaptive network of autonomous teams operating better in a complex and uncertain environment than a stable and predictable one. This approach allows individuals and teams in organizations to better self-control activities and obtain a higher sense of integration and self-satisfaction from them. Organic type of organization, with great autonomy in action, also allows better and faster adaptation to the frequently changing business environment. Autonomy in the organization does not imply independence from the environment, but the way its behaviors, decisions and other circumstances are determined by itself.
Holistic approach	Action philosophy	Existence of the organization is defined as a higher goal than only generation of profit and competition, in consequence, the terms competition and business are not attributed any great weight. The strength of the organization lies in its holism, a belief that it is impossible to learn all its forming phenomena, having an impact on it, if only its particular (selected) elements are taken into consideration.
	Leadership	A leader is forced to transfer leadership to the group, which a strong sense of community still connects him with. A leader is characterized by courage, humility and a level of top trust in relation to other persons and groups.
	Motivation	"Team spirit" is a factor motivating people to work, namely to make a shared effort for the fulfillment of the set tasks. The sense of community integrates the group, reduces stress and employees' extreme emotions.
	Communication	Free bottom-up flow of information in the organization, often being the basis for making centralized decisions.
	Operative model	High equality self-organizing teams. No management meetings. Projects implemented by particular employees, without supervision from the project leader. Transparent system of employee remuneration. Equal distribution of profit.
	Final results	Paradoxically, good results obtained by organizations, without any particular focus on business indicators.

(*Continued*)

Table 3.2 (*Continued*)

Paradigm	*Areas*	*Description*
Database approach*	Action philosophy	Organization operating in a data-based digital economy. Achieved results are a derivative of the skill of collecting, analyzing and processing data from various sources. Organizations typical of the behavioral model. Clear flattening of the organizational structures, including their decentralization and virtualization. Organization operating in a turbulent organizational environment, determined by technical innovations, rapidly changing goods and services. Strong integration of persons, machines, data and processes favors explosion of information later used by organizations to understand personalized customer needs.
	Leadership	Level of organizational flexibility directly correlated with the level of its leaders' agility. Strong emphasis on digital intelligence. Utilization of AI as a tool supporting management processes in the organization. Leadership requiring conceptual abilities, creative thinking and experimenting. Qualifications to manage teams composed both of persons and machines.
	Motivation	Motivating employees by setting more ambitious goals for them, expanding autonomy and experimenting in mastering in their work. New motivation is of critical importance for the future of organization and management.
	Communication	Large progress as compared to previous communication methods (including correctness of transmitted content) in the organization as a result of using artificial intelligence.
	Operative model	Project teams consisting of both persons and machines managed by the leader (triber). High autonomy of working with precisely specified tasks. Voluntary nature and trust in the organization in a digital economy favors creation of virtual structures. Management by algorithms.
	Final results	The organization's success is dependent on the skill of utilizing the possessed data resources.

Source: Prepared by the authors with the use of Hartikainen and Virtanen (2019).
* approach proposed by the authors of this book.

analysis and interpretation skills, and the organization's strategy to postmodern requirements. In the case of strategy, attention should be paid to ensure that it is focused not only on the organization's database resources, but also on human resources. In fact, machines (robots) will never replace people (workers), but can only help them in daily work, especially when it consists of collecting, processing and analyzing large data quantities.

Apart from administration and organization of work, transformations will also encompass the present management practices and models in the area of employee motivation. Revolutions, especially those related to new technologies, are characterized by a collective sense of willingness to change, frequently caused among societies accompanied by a strong motivation to pursue a better life. This means that other factors will motivate people to work in the AI era, compared to the very recent computerization era. Thus, this situation creates the need to change organizations' previous thinking about human motivation methods. Money, independence or awards will be necessary, but insufficient to persuade an employee to start work or make the decision to change it. The key to success, in the opinion of Pink (2009), will be **intrinsic motivation**.[4] In practice it will force organizations to build a work environment focused on three pillars: goal, autonomy and mastery. Goals, next to plans and intentions, are the condition that motivates people most to act and work intensely. Furthermore, more ambitious goals motivate undertaking an even greater effort. Therefore, organizations, in a personalized way, will be obliged to define goals for employees, which will reflect their personal ambitions as much as possible. In this way, organizations will be able to count on greater work commitment on the part of employees, which will essentially be a derivative of the progress they make. Also, a broad autonomy of teams is supposed to support fulfillment of goals. More often than before, they will independently make decisions in the organization and take full responsibility for them. In practice, this means that managers will make fewer decisions than even just recently. Any change in this area is caused by the evolution of organizational structures, which become increasingly unconventional and virtual. Therefore, greater autonomy in organizations will be consistent with the global trend related to changes in them. The last element in building internal motivation in the organization is, in the opinion of Pink, the pursuit of experiencing mastery in action. People naturally desire to be better, in particular in what they are doing. This approach to personal development has gained in importance, especially in today's world, where people are subjected to assessment, competition or comparisons from an early age. However, it is impossible to master work without the so-called flow,[5] a mental state when humans have the most clearly defined action goal and the final result is immediate as well as ideally having a correlation with his or her skills and capabilities. This means that an employee who will achieve such a state at work is not only more efficient but more satisfied. Making an analogy to the world of sport, it can be proposed that the success of the organization in the AI era will result from the combination of goals, ambitions and thinking of its employees.

The last presented management area that will be transformed by AI technology is leadership and operations (see Table 3.2). In the AI era, leadership, on the basis of the operations conducted, will be defined above all by any possessed abilities (including inborn intelligence, emotional and digital) to instantly involve networked teams (also composed of machines) that will have great autonomy and clearly defined action goals. This will take the form of shared leadership, with the beneficiaries being not only groups and teams, but all employees in the organization. On the other hand, current operations will be performed under the principles of self-management, without any intra-organizational hierarchy (virtual structures) and continuous search for acceptance of a consensus made within the team, or for a singlehandedly made decision. At the same time, Leadership 4.0 in the AI era will require capabilities of conceptual, systemic and graphic thinking, willingness to experiment, an ability to analyze data and efficiency in assessing their effect on people, digital abilities or a deep determination in pursuing success. The qualifications held by Leaders 4.0 will continue to be of prime importance from the point of view of management of teams, composed both of persons and machines.

General application technologies, and artificial intelligence should be regarded as such, next to the steam machine, internal combustion engine or electricity, have always been seen as the driving force of economic growth, but also as a catalyst for change. In management sciences such changes refer directly to an evolution of paradigms that define the way of planning, organizing, motivating and controlling activities and people in the organization. Bearing this in mind, it is difficult not to agree with the statement that the AI era will cause a permanent transformation in earlier thinking about the methods and the adopted management models. From the point of view of management, they will encompass a change of paradigms regarding:

- organizational structures, i.e. transition of organizations to non-hierarchical, virtual structures,
- organization's strategy, i.e. transition of organizations to data-based strategies,
- organizational environment, i.e. the organization's functioning in the digital economy era,
- intangible resources, i.e. treating data as the key asset in the organization,
- motivating, i.e. higher efficiency of the employees by intrinsic motivation,
- leadership, i.e. transition of organizations to shared leadership,
- management, i.e. transition of organizations to self-management,
- skills, namely their expansion in the organization to include digital abilities,
- abilities, i.e. their expansion in the organization to include digital intelligence,
- managing, i.e. transition to managing the works of teams consisting of people and machines,
- human resources, i.e. searching for employees with meta-skills.

3.3 Artificial intelligence in the organization – stages of implementation, assessment of resources, challenges

There are many reasons why entrepreneurs love AI, but one of the most important is that AI allows the organization to automate and optimize many business processes, increasingly also those more complex ones, often containing data in unstructured form. In addition, it serves to prepare new, personalized goods and business models, which at present, along with several other elements, are the hallmark of the **organization's digital maturity** – a process in which organizations are subjected to sustainable adaptation to the changing digital environment. However, actions related to planning, organizing and implementing AI in the organization not only require serious commitment and determination on the part of management, but often involve many obstacles. These are related to the shortage of a clearly defined strategy for AI, a shortage of people having relevant abilities to work in the AI environment on the labor market, a shortage of the necessary quantity of data and the technological infrastructure to operate AI, managers' concerns related to over-investment, a lack of framework that governs the functioning of AI, or a shortage of meaningful support from other organizations and state institutions. And even though the listed barriers strongly slow down the pace of implementing AI solutions in organizations, they do not discourage them from continuous actions taken to this end nor from asking important questions, e.g. how to adopt AI-based solutions in an organization. The answer to this question is multi-faceted, since it is a complicated matter related not only to the technology itself, but also to the entire organization and human expectations and actions. However, it should be honestly said that the implementation of AI is still, in many cases, a domain of large, rich transnational corporations, among which we can name: Google, Microsoft, Amazon, HSCB, Apple, General Electric, BMW, JP Morgan Chase, ICBC or Royal Dutch Shell. The reasons why these organizations have decided to implement AI are first of all related to the opportunities to obtain sustainable competitive advantage, faith in new development potential of their own business and expectations of customers who use AI-based goods. The dynamic development of AI worldwide makes this technology increasingly accessible, and thereby cheaper, also for a growing, broader group of other users. Smaller organizations also take advantage of it, as they are more willing to reach for AI technology, and the AI sector benefits most from this development, as on the global scale it is dynamically developing, and the organizations forming it are the elite of global innovation (see Table 3.3).

Bearing in mind the above-mentioned restrictions, managers intent on adopting AI solutions in their organization, must complete 15 tasks:

Task 1. Learn about AI.
Task 2. Ask questions about the operations of your organization and AI.
Task 3. Identify the "weak links" that AI may help you solve.
Task 4. Identify the value sources resulting from AI implementation.
Task 5. Identify the key processes in the organization.
Task 6. Identify the problem areas in which it will be possible to apply AI.
Task 7. Build a team composed of AI experts and specialists.
Task 8. Plan for AI training of your employees.
Task 9. Build a coherent AI strategy for your organization.
Task 10. Verify the amount and the quality of data in possession of your organization.
Task 11. Verify the technology available in the organization.
Task 12. Begin AI implementation without rush and in stages.
Task 13. Adapt AI to daily tasks.
Task 14. Campaign for the "connection" of the organization to a business ecosystem.
Task 15. In the field of AI, always act ethically.

In fact, the tasks proposed above are an attempt to present a staged approach to AI implementation in the organization. To assure their correctness, tasks must be

Table 3.3 The AI sector: 10 leading organizations in the world

Company	*Operations and flagship products*
AEye	AEye is an organization whose operations are based on building vision algorithms, computer software and hardware, which is later used to drive autonomous vehicles (driverless vehicles). The company uses and develops the laser scanning technology under the name LiDAR (Light Detection and Ranking), which allows acquisition of information about vehicle distances from people, other vehicles or animals, at the same time putting a smaller emphasis on such elements of the environment as buildings or vegetation.
AIBrain	AIBrain is a company offering artificial intelligence, which creates state-of-the-art solutions from this area for smartphones and the robotics sector. The primary goal of AIBrain's operations is development of works on a combination of artificial intelligence with human problem-solving, learning and memorizing skills.
AlphaSense	AlphaSense is an artificial intelligence-based search engine (using highly advanced search algorithms) designed for insurance, financial, investment companies, banks and companies from the Fortune 500 list. In practice these companies are looking for relevant information in transcripts regarding earnings, documents (catalogs) from stock exchanges or enterprises themselves. Companies can obtain such information primarily using the AI technology which makes more accurate data search possible by expanding it to include additional keywords for respective content.
Amazon	It is the best known worldwide online retail giant, founded in 1994 by Jeff Bezos, offering AI-based products and services to individual and retail customers. Among the flagship Amazon goods, we can mention for instance a whole product family Amazon Echo. In practice, it is an "intelligent" speaker connected to the Internet which we can control using our voice. It can put on music, ask for weather or add products to the wish list at Amazon. In addition, Amazon Echo it can be connected with any speaker supporting Bluetooth. Alexa SI is responsible for the operation of the device, a virtual personality operating in the cloud, which Amazon promotes as a competitor to Siri, produced by Apple Inc., namely an intelligent personal system.
Anki	Anki operates in one of the most rapidly developing robotics segments, consumer robotics (toys, education devices, household appliances, etc.). Anki constantly develops its flagship products in the form of Cozmo robot and the application Anki OVERDRIVE. Cozmo robot is one of the most sophisticated robots–consumer toys, showing its emotional reactions (through a layout of the eyes and the sounds made) to the environment and its forming elements. Cozmo robot bears a striking resemblance to toys from animated cartoons, e.g. Toy Story. As far as the application Anki OVERDRIVE is concerned, it is presently considered as the most intelligent racing system worldwide. In practice, it is a game, in which each car is a conscious, AI-powered robot equipped with a "killer" strategy based on the assumption: the better you play, the better you become.

(*Continued*)

Table 3.3 (*Continued*)

Company	*Operations and flagship products*
Blue River Tech	Blu River Tech, as a subsidiary of Deere & Co., in their work combines artificial intelligence with image processing and analysis (computer vision) in order to create smart farming technologies (SFT). One of Blu River Tech innovative technologies is See & Spray system which identifies single plants and applies herbicides (chemical products) only in the case of weeds. In practice this allows the quantity of sprayed chemicals to be reduced by as much as 90% as compared to the traditional methods.
Casetext	It is a company from San Francisco (United States), which has developed an artificial intelligence-based legal search engine specializing in identification, analysis and viewing of legal documents. The database where documents are searched contains over 10 million acts, orders, regulations and other legal acts. During recent research that was intended to compare among themselves any other platforms which lawyers most frequently use in their work, it turned out that the people who used Casetext CARA A.I: first of all, dedicated 25% less time for their job; second, could perform a smaller number of searches, to find respective documents; and, third, in almost 20% of the cases, their search was more appropriate than that made on other platforms.
Cogni-tiveScale	The company creates AI-based applications for customer service departments in companies from the banking, insurance, financial and investment sectors. In addition, CognitiveScale solutions are used in the medical industry to manage patient services. The company's products are based on an augmented intelligence platform named Cortex which is available for other specialists daily involved in the broadly defined AI.
Clarifai	Clarifai is a company with a registered office in New York, which deals with artificial intelligence. Its flagship product is a platform for recognition, filtering and searching a large database containing various images. The platform has been designed to ensure a possibility for finding similarities in the images searched.
CloudMinds	CloudMinds, as the first company worldwide, develops a comprehensive ecosystem for the operation of cloud-connected smart machines. With its main product, HARI platform (Human Augmented Robotics Intelligence), the company, in the real time, supports world class operators in the production of AI-based robots. In other words, CloudMinds combines a machine (robot) with the person allowing, when necessary, the robot to be controlled by the person.

Source: Authors' own study on the basis of Patrizio (2019).

implemented in the appropriate order. The interpretation of each of the 15 tasks is as follows.

3.3.1 Learn AI

Before starting an "adventure" with AI, time should be spent to become familiar with its contemporary possibilities. In fact, contrary to common thinking, AI is a concept that has been developed for 70 years worldwide (see Table 2.3 in Chapter 2). Therefore, it may boast of significant achievements, both in science and in practice. The knowledge should be obtained from different available sources, including Internet AI platforms, online courses, open-source Internet libraries, or AI strategies which have already been prepared and published by countries (in particular highly developed nations) around the world. Particular attention should be paid to AI tools (see Chapter 2.2), the dynamic development of which has contributed to its global popularization.

3.3.2 *Ask questions about the operations of your organization and AI*

The AI implementation process in the organization should be preceded by an attempt to ask key questions and look for answers to them regarding how we work, what our activities mostly focus on, how we enter into interactions with the customer or with our partners, what our strengths and weaknesses are, etc. These questions should be constantly supplemented with others, including those related to our examinations regarding the practical use of AI in the organization with reference to people, processes, operations, data and technologies.

3.3.3 *Identify the "weak links" that AI may help you solve*

The next step is attempted identification of these areas in the organization where the possibility of AI application will contribute to growth in the added value of the goods manufactured or the services provided. Thus, the specific cases should be examined where AI can be used as a tool to support, improve or solve a given business problem, at the same time creating added value. The opportunities of using AI-based solutions, it is worth remembering, will always depend on the specific nature of a particular industry.

3.3.4 *Identify the value sources resulting from AI implementation*

AI can create value in many business areas of the organization, therefore, they should all be thoroughly examined. With value created by AI, organizations forecast demand better, manage their inventory more effectively, reduce the costs of their operations faster, increasing their income, and, in consequence, also profits. Their market offers are better adapted to consumer locations, tastes and preferences. Therefore, high personalization of products and services favors increased loyalty on the part of their users. The fulfillment of this task should always be focused on combining business ideas and initiatives with the possibilities of achieving specific values.

3.3.5 *Identify the key processes in the organization*

The identification of core business processes in the organization is primarily about finding opportunities for their automation (if not completed yet). It is a good moment before final AI implementation. The digital economy and its progress will impose growing pressure on organizations to make any processes performed faster and more effective.

3.3.6 Identify the problem areas in which it will be possible to apply AI

The problem areas that are part of the space of the entire organization are primarily characterized by the fact that they cause certain anomalies, both for the internal and external environment of the organization. Therefore, they must be thoroughly recognized and then, considering that they challenge the pursuit of organizational objectives, a choice should be made to subject them to AI solutions.

3.3.7 Build a team composed of AI experts and specialists and plan AI training of your employees

Building a team of experts as well as persons knowledgeable in AI is one of the key challenges faced by an organization wanting to implement AI-based technologies. The problem of an educational gap existing in this area results in the organization not being able to focus only on external recruitment, the more so since it is often a costly and largely risky process. Moreover, the demand on the labor market for AI specialists clearly exceeds supply. Everything indicates that this situation will continue for several years. For this reason, the organization must also, and perhaps and first of all, focus on educating and training its employees. This training should be done by experts with great knowledge in AI and its constituent elements. In fact, the accumulation of AI knowledge makes managers better able to manage their expectations, as they will have knowledge of what AI can and cannot do under specific conditions for the organization. The internal raising of the employee qualifications, while not replacing many years of specialist education and experts' experience, can prove effective in limiting the problems the organization is facing due to a shortage of AI professionals on the labor market. Furthermore – in the long term – internal AI training can be attractive for the employees, in particular from the point of view of their personal development and professional loyalty.

3.3.8 Plan for AI training of your employees

AI training courses that an organization plans for its employees should be carefully prepared and defined: the subject area, target groups and goal they should achieve. In particular, it should be considered whether training in the field of AI will be addressed to: all people, beginners, senior management or managers interested in AI implementations.

3.3.9 Build a coherent AI strategy for your organization

Adaptation of AI-based solutions in an organization must be preceded by preparation of the right strategy in this regard. Its construction is one of the most important tasks faced by the management of any business wanting to gain the title of an

AI-based organization in the future. The AI strategy must inform all the organization's stakeholders about the direction it will follow. Furthermore, it must specify the abilities of creative cooperation with other entities for which the AI concept is the driving force of development. However, creating a strategy in the area of AI requires managers to deeply understand this technology, and especially its abilities and "natural" limitations. In addition, it is necessary to define a set of criteria and decision-making rules that will shape the functioning and development of the organization in the AI environment. In practice, this means that the implementation of AI requires a strategic approach, the setting of general and detailed goals, identification of key performance indicators and tracking of the return on investment in AI. Lack of a clear strategy and an adequate approach to it may complicate, and in many cases also prevent, effective AI implementation in the organization.

3.3.10 Verify the amount and the quality of data being in the possession of your organization

In order to maximize the benefits arising from AI implementation in the organization, its management must change the approach not only to people and processes but also to the data itself. To be valuable from the point of view of AI, data must not only come from proper sources but must also be of proper quality. This means that it must be up-to-date and consistent as well as structured (ordered). The management of the organization should thus aim to identify and integrate high quality data sets that can then be applied in sales, production, customer relations or financial management systems.

3.3.11 Verify the technology available in the organization

To ensure that AI implementation will end successfully for the organization, take a close look at the technology that is currently used in it. This means verifying the number of tasks, services, processes, what type (simple, complex), in which areas of the organization, with the application of which technology, are automated. It should be remembered that a higher degree of automation of actions favors easier adaptation of the AI environment in the organization, and vice versa.

3.3.12 Begin AI implementation without rush and in stages

AI implementation in the organization should proceed gradually and in a well-thought-out manner. This implies that in the era of continuous rush and stress, omitting any of the stages related to AI implementation may expose the organization not only to losses, but above all to excessive delays. These may result in reducing its competitive advantage on the market as compared to other companies that are systematically, step by step, pursuing the AI implementation strategy.

Bearing this in mind managers in organizations should thoroughly plan and analyze stages of its adaptation.

3.3.13 Adapt AI to everyday tasks

Because many people distrust AI, fearing, among other things, that it can deprive them of work, therefore they are reluctant to engage in initiatives related to it. A good way to change employees' approach to AI-based solutions is their gradual familiarization with the benefits that it can offer them in daily work. If the AI technology becomes a routine tool in their work, then they will not perceive it as an "unwanted alternative". Therefore, managers in the organization should focus on assuring that AI becomes perceived by the employees as a helpful tool, a necessary supplement to their work.

3.3.14 Campaign for the organization's "connection" to a business ecosystem

The problems faced today by managers in organizations that are focused on AI technology implementation, concerning the shortage of specialists, experts, knowledge and directional support, add to the difficulty of AI implementation. To overcome these difficulties, or most of them, the organization's management should solicit its connection with a business ecosystem. This unique type of a cooperation and partnership network based on innovation and co-evolution is a good platform for stimulating progress related to AI implementation in a given organization. In fact, the strength of a business ecosystem is in the direct exchange of knowledge and experience of its participating stakeholders.

3.3.15 In the field of AI, always act ethically

When adopting AI technology-based solutions in the organization we should not forget about their ethical dimension. The management model the organization follows and the values it promotes should never be in conflict with the AI concept. Thus, teams cooperating with AI must never have a sense of being subject to surveillance, having no privacy or lack of understanding for their problems. For this reason, the organization should establish a code of ethical practice in the context of the tasks performed with the participation of AI.

For managers in the organization the tasks presented above can be a unique type of a road map in the implementation of AI technology in organizations. And even though these tasks are not exhaustive in view of the whole spectrum of actions necessary to be carried out in this area, they are undoubtedly a significant part of it. In addition, it should be mentioned that since every organization is different (has a different management model and promotes different values), each can experience the AI adaptation process in a different way. However, some problems, regardless of the size or nature of the organization, will be identical, especially in the area of human resources or large data resources. Therefore, AI implementation in the organization should be preceded by a deep analysis of its resources and possibilities.

3.4 AI organizations – a new type of organization in the world of management

AI-based solutions have become almost omnipresent. In assisting human actions, AI today makes decisions related to the most diverse aspects of life, from problems related to granting a bank loan, to predictions concerning a person's health or life span. Therefore, the revolution caused by the development of AI brings along a fundamental change to the pace of life and lifestyle as well as its quality and the value systems carried within it. Apart from people, transformation affects other aspects of life, social, cultural, international, legal or economic. In the context of the latter, the transformation taking place in the environment of the organization seems to be especially important, where earlier management models are gradually being substituted by new, postmodern ones. This means that AI has broad and deep implications for everybody involved in business management. Organizations also gain a new shape and character and, driven by AI, increasingly often call themselves AI-based organizations or AI organizations.[6]

From the definition-based point of view, **AI organizations** should be considered those that concentrate their efforts on research and development focused on creating products based on solutions in the field of machine learning, whose stream of revenue is mostly based on such applications (Lorenz & Saslow, 2019). Surprisingly, the definition above is one of few that we can encounter in publications devoted to AI. Due to this fact, the authors of the study have decided to present their own proposals explaining the essence of this term. Therefore, adopting as the criterion the scope of the services provided, AI organizations should include those that offer their customers solutions based on: artificial intelligence, the Internet of Things, machine learning, business process automation, mobile application development, data set analysis, computational cloud or blockchain technology. In another, more synthetic, sense, AI organizations can be defined as market entities that use cognitive (learning) technologies in their everyday work, concerning, e.g. AI, machine learning or robotics, to expand and enhance human intelligence, which in turn is to contribute to discovering new business opportunities for the organization. In the functional perspective, AI organizations should be perceived as business operations focused on sale of products and services the technology of which is based on AI. Finally, in the conceptual perspective, AI organizations can be defined as planned projects with a well-thought-out man–machine–work environment design, which, using the basic cognitive tools and data resources, pursue their goals, building new offers and business models. A common feature of the presented definitions of the term AI organization is that each of them, not always in a direct way, talks about the benefits arising from a creative combination of human work (person) with innovative technology (machine). Apart from that, it should be mentioned that each such organization treats data acquisition as a strategic goal, which essentially is to strengthen human intelligence in the organization (including human efficiency) in cooperation with digital machines.

Bearing in mind the above-mentioned definitions and the conditions related to the AI organization's access to basic input information, which is necessary for algorithms to find a solution (generate a result), Lorenz and Saslow (2019) distinguish three basic types:

- AI organizations at the initial stage of development (early stages ventures),
- AI organizations based on AI domain specific application,
- AI platforms.

According to the authors, the difference between these organizations is primarily caused by their access to the main components that "comprise" AI and which refer to data, software, computer hardware or human potential[7] as well as the possibility of their combined application. However, in this latter case, its realization requires access both to financial capital and expert technical knowledge.

When it comes to **AI organizations** that are **at the initial stage of development** (often in the foundation phase), they are characterized by a low degree of digitization, basic analytical potential, performance of tasks and ideas with the use of basic elements of the machine learning technology utilizing basic algorithmics as well as a low level of seed capital both in the tangible and intangible form. At this level, AI organizations are looking for talents in the AI area, promoting ideas of a data-driven organization and exploring knowledge related to AI in order to use it in practice. Knowledge expansion results from intensive development of cooperation with science institutions, research and development networks or universities. In practice, AI organizations, in the initial phase of their development, frequently have the status of startup organizations. For them the key element is to expand access to subsequent data sets that are a *sine qua non* condition of their further development. Such organizations also require permanent supervision from management staff, because their evolution in the area of innovation affects the level of attracted capital, which is necessary in the process of their transformation into more mature forms of AI-based organizations. A higher level of technological sophistication in the AI arena is demonstrated by **domain-based AI organizations and artificial intelligence applications**. While they have most of the attributes which are typical of AI organizations at the initial stage of development, they are distinguished by several additional aspects. First, these are organizations which, as part of research and development activities already performed for a long time, create their own products and services using artificial intelligence technology and the machine learning technology for this purpose. This allows them to generate a high stream of revenues thanks to their own solutions. Second, they demonstrate a "higher culture" of data, which are of high quality, organized, grouped and, importantly, refer to the knowledge resources in the particular industry. Third, artificial intelligence technology is introduced to the organization's many strategic initiatives and projects, intended to support increased work efficiency and the creation of new approaches and business models (Middleton et al., 2019). Fourth, such organizations are pursuing joint venture capital projects, which are based on research partnerships that group stakeholders from different sectors of the economy. Fifth, a strong concentration of management staff on recruitment of AI talents and experts is typical. And sixth, in the opinion of Lorenz and Saslow (2019) AI organizations that every day use AI technology and machine learning in an advanced way, are willing, for the purpose of further expansion of their specialist knowledge, to take over other "competent" entities. The last type of AI organization are the **AI platforms**. These are organizations which, from the point of view of self-development and artificial intelligence technologies, have undergone a cultural transformation. They are characterized by having devices with huge computational powers helping them to quickly process and store large data collections. In addition, they possess a high number of tools that allow development of smart applications. Thanks to an appropriate combination of smart decision-making algorithms with data, AI platforms also generate new business models and solutions, which later reach the market in the form of finished products or services. As organizations, AI platforms are also a key element in **innovation ecosystems** (see Figure 3.2), namely environments that create new values in the process of transforming new ideas and projects into real goods. The strength of partnership and cooperation in an ecosystem is so large, that the forming community reciprocally supports its objectives, missions, visions and

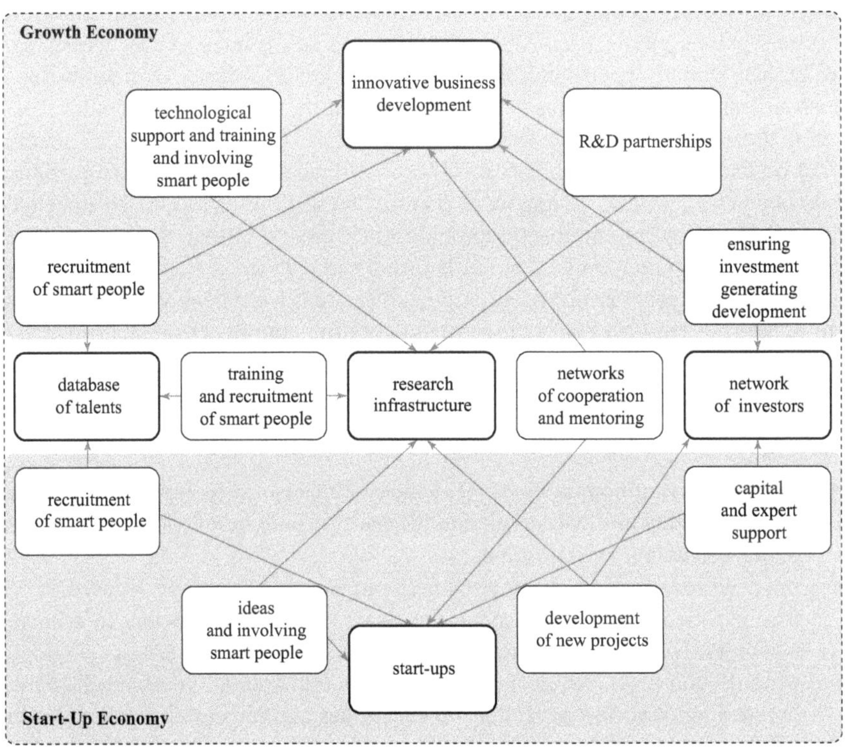

Figure 3.2 The innovation ecosystem – a graphic example. Source: Based on Morrison (2016).

values, which it pursues and follows. An important feature that distinguishes AI platforms from other organizations is that, caring for the safety of their innovation bases, they create their own (internal) research and development centers. The most important ones worth mentioning are Google Brain,[8] Facebook AI Research, Baidu Research or Alibaba Damo[9] (Lorenz & Saslow, 2019).

Although the types of AI organizations presented above differ from each other in terms of the level of growth, access to key artificial intelligence components, models of the adopted development strategy as well as the potential to obtain large sets of precise data, in the opinion of Lorenz and Saslow (2019) they share two characteristics that qualify them for the group of AI organizations. The first is a strong focus on operations and cooperation in the field of research and development, with the participation of research institutes, universities and other research centers. The second is that a significant revenue stream in these organizations is generated by selling their own AI-based products and services. Still one more characteristic should be added to this set of common, or distinguishing features of AI organizations, namely the creation of organizational structures consisting of multi-disciplinary teams. In fact, AI development generates a range of multi-dimensional tasks and projects, that the traditional approach to the design of organizational structures would ascribe an insufficient adaptability of the organization to changes taking place in a world based on algorithms, digitization or, more broadly, digitalization. Although AI technology is increasingly accessible, which also directly contributes to its (gradually lower) prices, AI organizations must still spend large amounts of funds to continue their development on this market. In the opinion of analysts from International Data Corporation (IDC)[10] in only 2021 organizations will spend nearly USD 60 billion on AI and machine learning. It is beyond doubt that a significant share of these funds will also be intended for actions related to employee retraining, the more so in that shortages in this area, especially with regard to the skills associated with the proficient use of tools in robotics and programming, are large enough that specialists with such skills are presently (that is in 2020) the most sought-after employees on labor markets worldwide. But implications and challenges on the part of AI both for the organization and societies until at least 2029 will increase in number and, in the opinion of Kelner and Kostadinov (2019), they will be concerned with the following:

- further growing popularity of AI, which will cause shifts in value chains of various sectors and will accelerate the pace of both innovation and creative disruption among organizations,
- the need to transform present business models, which will be focused more than before on new competences, necessary for the organizations to achieve a competitive position on markets,
- benefits and risks for societies related to transformation of health care, broadening of access to products and services and increased productivity in industry and agriculture, growing automation increasing inequalities among nations and societies, greater surveillance and development of conflicts with possible use of Lethal Autonomous Weapon Systems, LAWS.[11]

3.5 Data as the strategic resource of the organization in the AI era

The open data economy is the next evolutionary development stage of the global economy, after the resource-based economy or knowledge-based economy. Contrary to previous periods, it is not the natural resources (land and minerals), tangible (capital) or human resources (employees), but those related to data collections[12] that are presently regarded in the economy as most important. They give rhythm to the factors shaping the structure of modern manufacturing and social and economic progress worldwide. Furthermore, the geometric pace of their growth brings transformation not only to small organizations and groups of people, but also to large corporations or nations. The open data economy, being the fourth stage of digitization development,[13] is thus evolving at a staggering pace. As an example, it is worth mentioning the scale of digital data flow for the global online traffic, which has increased since 2002 from about 100 GB[14] per second to 46 000 GB per second in 2017, and in 2022, as indicated by forecasts, will reach the level of 150 700 GB per second (Sirimanne et al., 2019). However, from the macroeconomic, but also the microeconomic, point of view, what is important for the development of both the economy and the organization is not so much the data volume as their quality. In practice, it is mostly perceived through the prism of usability, correctness, integrity, consistency or timelessness of data. Their processing, and then being used for manufacturing purposes by various entities may not, however, ignore their type. The point is to know whether the data the organization uses are:

- private or public,
- open or secret,
- operational or strategic,
- personalized or general,
- sensitive or insensitive,
- ordinary personal data or special category personal data.

Any lack of knowledge in this area may result in the organization being:

- exposed to the risk of making incorrect decisions,
- exposed to the risk of loss of reputation and trust among the stakeholders,
- exposed to the risk of civil and legal liability,
- exposed to the risk of loss of revenue in future periods,
- exposed to the risk of building products and services which may constitute a threat to health and life of individuals,
- exposed to the risk of unethical behaviors.

All this contributes to the constantly growing impact (both positive as well as negative one) of increasing data volumes on organizations, the more so that the number of data worldwide (on the market) is growing rather than decreasing. We are already dealing with not so much duplication as multiplication. Creating **data from data** is no longer a rare practice, but the daily life of many organizations for which this is their core business. However, it should be emphasized here that the data which at present are perceived by AI organizations as a valuable asset are not something new for them, because they have accompanied the development of the operations conducted for a long time. A novelty is that they originate from new end points, such as Internet of Things (IoT) devices, which increase the number of available data (Opher et al., 2016). Therefore, their proper use can serve the organization to either significantly reduce costs related to the operations being conducted, or to create new opportunities and achieve additional value that will support the creation of new ideas and new competitive advantages on the market (see Table 3.4). In this case, we are talking not only about the perspective related to the organization's potential to create new products and services, but also the

Table 3.4 Examples of cost reductions and value creation in organizations with the use of data from IoT devices

The use of data from the Internet of Things to reduce costs in the organization	*The use of data from the Internet of Things to achieve value in the organization*
Workforce efficiency increases by implementing automation, improved visibility and early identification of irregularities (anomalies) by means of analyses.	Possible data monetization by selling the organization's data or licensing taxonomy.
Higher supply chain efficiency thanks to data from sensors in production halls and vehicles. Possible elimination of unnecessary activities performed by the personnel and optimization of transport routes.	Bettering (processing) of existing products and services, thanks to analyzing data from purchased products.
Safety improvement thanks to synchronization of the equipment, personnel and location data.	Identification of new applications and software for existing products and services.
Limitation of production and design defects with the use of data from embedded sensors to conduct malfunction analyses and failure risk level analyses (e.g. parametric analysis, degradation analysis).	Mark-ups on existing products are growing, and new products are launched to the market by assimilation of data in the process.
Building optimization reduces the costs of energy consumption, its maintenance and management. Generally, an improvement is made in care for the organization's assets.	Product placement, store layouts, marketing and consumers' general impression are improved as a result of new data as well as extensive analyses.
Improvement in using resources as a result of monitoring equipment. Application of manufacturing sensors reduces maintenance costs, costs of used resources, reduces the level of breakdowns, defects or downtimes in the production process.	*Pay-per-use* service as well as setting service prices are possible owing to data collection.

Source: Own study based on Opher et al. (2016).

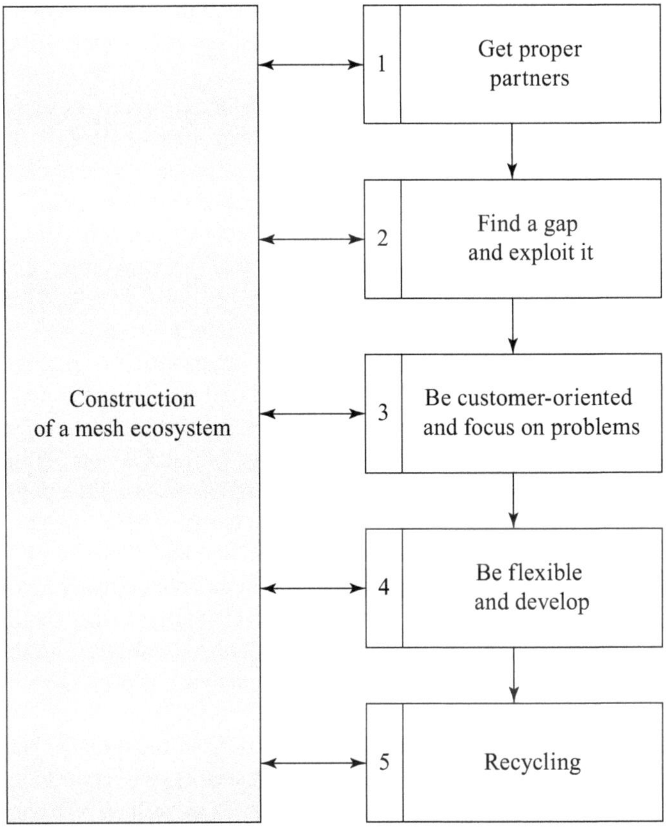

Figure 3.3 Basic elements of a mesh ecosystem. Source: Based on BusinessNews Publishing (2014).

initiation of unique solutions, for example creating **mesh ecosystems**. In practice, they are built through close cooperation of many entities (stakeholders) and items (equipment, machines), which through the systems for exchange of information and effective use of the available resources, create deeply integrated networks between partners operating within the ecosystem.

In the opinion of Gansky (2010), for organizations to create a stable and actively operating mesh ecosystem requires the integration of five key elements (see Figure 3.3):

- **acquisition of proper business partners** – a characteristic feature of mesh ecosystems is that they function on the principle of shared decision-making and shared management. In practice, this means that the whole mesh is managed not by one, but by many people. Thus, partners in such an ecosystem can be successful in large part due to capabilities they have in communication, sharing knowledge, collaboration and coordination of the tasks being performed. In addition, it is necessary to integrate IT systems, to ensure that all the partners creating the mesh could have insight into the same information that will be the basis for creating new products, providing innovative services and setting common development strategies,

- **identification of a market niche and exploiting it before competitors** – the point is to recognize customer tastes and exactly identify their needs. In fact, market niches demonstrate high potential both in terms of generating additional income and value as well as satisfying the most sophisticated customer tastes,
- **focus on customers and their problems** – with reference to an ecosystem, the idea is that its organization takes account of the areas serving customers in solving their daily problems or concerns,
- **skills in flexible adaptation to the changing environment** – in practice, it is a crucial factor for the future development of the organization or partner cooperation networks. In other words, one cannot build a solid mesh ecosystem that would be non-flexible and would adjust with difficulty to the dynamically changing environment, customer tastes or current fashion. Mesh ecosystems foster solutions, which can be described as innovative, little popularized, highly personalized and quickly evolving in terms of development,
- **avoidance of wastage** – to be understood not only as reduction in the quantity of waste, but also resignation from everything that in an economically irrational manner may contribute to ineffective use of available resources (both limited and unlimited ones), the more so that an immanent feature of mesh ecosystems is avoidance of mismanagement through network supervision.

Here it should be noted that not only the above-mentioned mesh ecosystems, but synthetically speaking, all ecosystems (related to different sectors) will contribute both to enhancing the development of data-based economies as well as building the organizations' new business models of cooperation between their stakeholders. Moreover, the cooperation ecosystems–organizations will be conducive to generation of new ideas and further data. In practice, this means that organizations must think about the potential to use them. Depending on the scale, perhaps it will even be necessary to reorganize the organizational structure of an enterprise so as to better adjust it to the changing environment.

Bearing in mind the above, it should be stated that to succeed in the AI era, the data the organization has and manages must be properly processed, at every stage of performing a particular task, project or implementing an idea. Proper (or exemplary) data processing in the organization can be a situation where they are profiled according to the stages related to (see Figure 3.4):

- data acquisition,
- obtaining access to data,
- data storage,
- data validation,
- data standardization,
- data visualization.

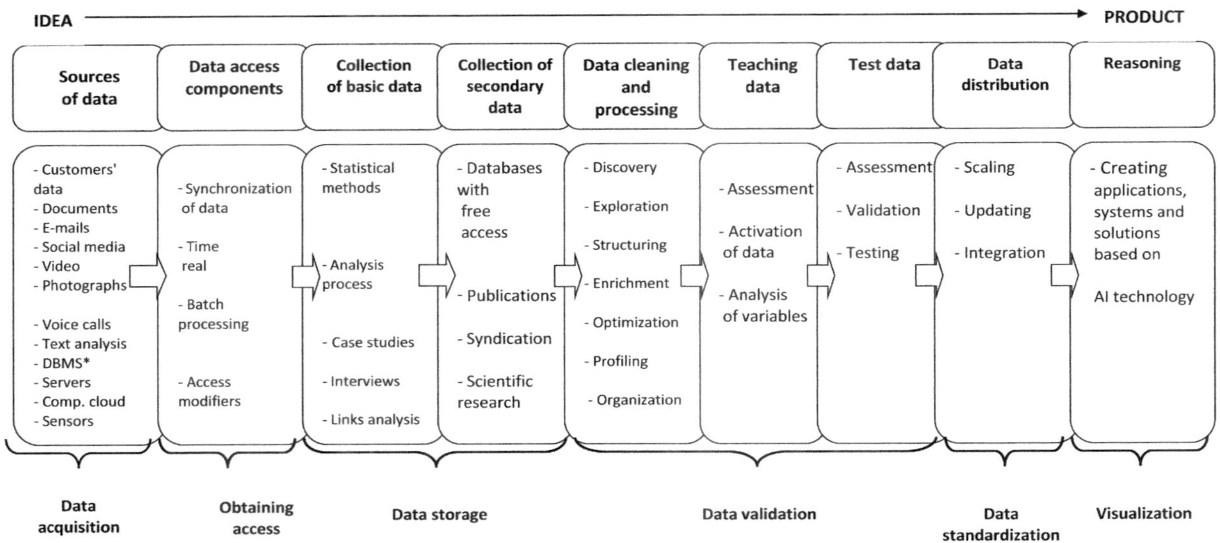

Figure 3.4 Model of data processing in AI technology-based organizations. Note: *Database Management System – systems for management of databases. Source: Prepared by the authors.

Here, once again, what has been written earlier should be emphasized: what is important is not data quantity, but quality and the value for the organization. Therefore, proper data processing is conducive to highlighting their quality which, indirectly, should be understood as the strength that data has in technological and social innovation, creation of new market niches or modern business solutions.

In the context of the approach to data presented above that organizations manifest in the era of AI technology, a question arises: why are they so important for them? The search for an answer seems to be more complex than it may seem at first sight and results mostly from the multi-faceted nature and the importance of data for the organization. **First**, it should be noticed that we live in the era of the data-driven economy, which is essentially the next stage of the evolutionary development of the world economy. In practice, this means that countries in general and organizations in particular are the primary generators of data which are then used as the basic resource in the production and development of AI technology-based tools. **Second**, today organizations perceive data as a fundamental element in creating their business processes and strategies. **Third**, mutual penetration and supplementation of data from various sources is perceived by various entities as a valuable asset that, when properly utilized, can be used to build competitive advantage on the market. **Fourth**, data, in particular non-structured, are easily accessible and cheap. **Fifth**, the value of working with data centers on the employees in the organization who, with the use of business intelligence applications, have the ability to perform complex data analyses (see Table 3.5), which then become the basis for making operating and strategic decisions in the organization. **Sixth**, completeness of data allows the management to build a holistic image of the organization, which will also highlight its strengths and weaknesses. **Seventh**, data allow the organization to continuously improve their products and services, and in this way increase customer satisfaction, boost sales profitability and strengthen the company's market position. **Eighth**, with data possessed by the organization, it is possible to analyze current and historical facts, in order to make predictions (see predictive algorithms, Chapter 2.5). **Ninth**, data are the basic component, by means of which the organization's stakeholders make an assessment of the teams' work and the functioning of the organization as a whole. And **tenth**, data is key to optimizing processes inside the organization. In practice, as a result of the growing measurement of processes and their increased degree of automation, organizations have detailed information on how they proceed and function. As a result, it is possible to build process models with the use of predictive analysis.

Finally, it is worth pointing out that, in spite of the production of large data volumes, gradual standardization of the ways of their processing or AI organizations' growing attention, data across the world are only utilized to a small extent. This situation means that particular countries and organizations increasingly often compete for them, while simultaneously participating in a race the purpose of which is to define the future paradigm of the data-based economy.

Table 3.5 Selected best Business Intelligence (BI) applications in 2020 – comparison

Name of BI application \ *BI functions*	*Adaptive Insights*	*Board*	*Dundas BI*	*WebFOCUS*	*Sisense*	*Looker*	*Hubble*	*Zoho Analytics*	*TapClicks*
Country of origin (a)	US	CH	CA	US	IL	US	US	US	US
Analysis *ad hoc*	✓	✓	✓	✓	✓	✓	✓	✓	✗
Inquiries *ad hoc*	✓	✓	✓	✓	✓	✓	✓	✓	✗
Reports *ad hoc*	✓	✓	✓	✓	✓	✓	✓	✓	✓
Benchmarking	✓	✓	✓	✓	✓	✓	✗	✗	✗
Budgeting and prediction	✓	✓	✓	✓	✓	✓	✓	✗	✗
Scoreboard (b)	✓	✓	✓	✓	✓	✓	✓	✓	✓
Data analysis	✓	✓	✓	✓	✓	✓	✓	✓	✓
Data visualization	✓	✓	✓	✓	✓	✓	✓	✓	✓
KPI (c)	✓	✓	✓	✓	✓	✓	✓	✓	✗
OLAP (d)	✓	✓	✓	✓	✓	✗	✗	✗	✗
Performance ratios (e)	✓	✓	✓	✓	✓	✓	✓	✓	✗
Predictive analysis	✓	✓	✓	✓	✗	✗	✓	✓	✗
Profitability analysis	✓	✓	✓	✓	✓	✓	✓	✓	✗
Strategic planning	✓	✓	✓	✓	✓	✓	✓	✗	✗
Trend/problem indicators	✓	✓	✓	✓	✓	✓	✓	✗	✗

Source: Own study based on softwareworld.co.
(a): IL-Israel, US-United States, CH-Switzerland, CA-Canada.
(b): dashboard.
(c): Key Performance Indicators.
(d): On-Line Analytical Processing.
(e): Performance Metrics.

Notes

1 Elon Musk is a businessman and philanthropist from South Africa. As a visionary he has created several companies, including SpaceX, Tesla, The Boring Company or Neuralink. For many years, he has been involved in projects that may in the future turn out to be groundbreaking for humanity. SpaceX is currently working on sending people to Mars, creating an interplanetary travel system or delivering satellites to the Earth's orbit. In the case of Tesla, works are underway to launch autonomous vehicles, while at Neuralink experts are working on an enigmatic project, with the goal being to connect the human brain with a computer.
2 The questionnaire survey was completed on a group of 2500 directors and managers, with support of 17 expert surveys.
3 The first edition of the book was published in 1962.
4 So far, employers have mostly seen external factors as the basic sources for motivating employees.
5 A concept created by Hungarian psychologist Mihály Csíkszentmihályi.
6 In publications devoted to AI or Industry 4.0, we also come across the term "organizations of tomorrow".
7 In the future, it should be expected that these components will perhaps be supplemented by biological systems (wetware) or chemical systems (chemware).

8 This is an artificial intelligence research team, created in 2010 in California by Google. The operations of the research and development center focus on a combination of research in machine learning with advanced engineering of systems and computational resources, within the operations of the entire organization. One of the latest Google Brain studies is the creation of a program which learns to code itself. In this way, in the developers' work, writing or modifying code would proceed automatically, with the use of machine learning and neural networks technologies.
9 This is a science and research center, created in 2017 for USD 15 billion by Alibaba. The second part of this center's name, Damo, is the acronym from the words: Discovery, Adventure, Momentum and Outlook. An interesting fact is that the center has offices at different places worldwide, where the best AI specialists can be employed. Currently Alibaba Damo has offices in Beijing and Hangzhou (China), Singapore (Singapore), Seattle, Sunnyvale as well as New York (United States) and Tel Aviv (Israel).
10 IDC is a global, leading supplier of market data, advisory services as well as events on the ICT services market. The organization operates in more than 110 countries across the world. For more information, see: www.idc.com.
11 For more information, see: Lele (2019).
12 Often, especially in the professional literature, large-scale data storage is called a data lake. This applies both to structured data, half-structured and non-structured data.
13 For more information, see: https://www.gov.pl/web/cyfryzacja/industry.
14 Gigabytes.

References

Aon. (2019). *The Future of Business: How Artificial Intelligence Can Drive Organizational Change*. TheOneBrief. Downloaded 20 November 2019 from: https://theonebrief.com/the-future-of-business-how-artificial-intelligence-can-drive-organizational-change/.

BusinessNews Publishing. (2014). *Summary: The Mesh: Review and Analysis of Gansky's Book*. Troy, MI: Primento.

Gansky, L. (2010). *The Mesh: Why the Future of Business Is Sharing*. New York: Portfolio Penguin.

Hartikainen, J., & Virtanen, M. (2019). Management paradigms in a nutshell. Downloaded 30 November 2019 from: https://www.tieto.com/en/blog/2019/07/management-paradigms-in-a-nutshell/.

Kelner, D., & Kostadinov, A. (2019). *The State of AI 2019: Divergence*. London: MMC Ventures Research.

Kolbjørnsrud, V., Amico, R., & Thomas, R. J. (2016a). How artificial intelligence will redefine management. *Harvard Business Review*. Downloaded 1 December 2019 from: https://hbr.org/2016/11/how-artificial-intelligence-will-redefine-management.

Kolbjørnsrud, V., Amico, R., & Thomas, R. J. (2016b). *The Promise of Artificial Intelligence. Redefining Management in the Workforce of the Future*. Oslo: Accenture.

Lele, A. (2019). Debating lethal autonomous weapon systems. Institute for defence studies and analyses. *J. Def. Stud.*, *13*(1), January–March, pp. 51–70.

Lorenz, P., & Saslow, K. (2019). *Demystifying AI & AI Companies. What Foreign Policy Makers Need to Know about the Global AI Industry*. Berlin: Stiftung Neue Verantwortung e.V.

Middleton, J., McCahon, W., Rosenshine, K., Jonem, J., Cawthorne, H., & Duncan, A. (2019). *Artificial Intelligence in Financial Services*. London: UK Finance.

Morrison, E (2016). *Moving our Innovation Thinking from Barriers to Ecosystems.* Florence, AL: Agile Strategy Lab Network, University and the University of North Alabama.

Opher, A., Chou, A., Onda, A., & Sounderrajan, K. (2016). *The Rise of the Data Economy: Driving Value through Internet of Things Data Monetization.* A Perspective for Chief Digital Officers and Chief Technology Officers. New York: IBM Global Services.

Patrizio, A. (2019). These artificial intelligence companies are advancing this emerging tech through myriad developments of AI systems. Downloaded 4 November 2019 from: https://www.datamation.com/artificial-intelligence/top-artificial-intelligence-companies.html.

Pink, D. H. (2009). *Drive: The Surishing Truth About What Motivates Us.* New York: Riverhead Books.

Ransbotham, S., Khodabandeh, S., Fehling, R., LaFountain, B., & Kiron, D. (2019). *Winning With AI. Pioneers Combine Strategy, Organizational Behavior, and Technology.* Cambridge, MA: MIT Sloan Management Review and Boston Consulting Group.

Schatsky, D., Camhi, J., & Muraskin, C. (2019). *Data Ecosystems: How Third-Party Information Can Enhance Data Analytics.* New York: National Office; Deloitte Development LLC.

Sirimanne, S. N., Fredriksson, T., Fajarnes-Garces, P., Fondeur-Gil, S., Jones, Ch., Julsaint-Kidane, M., Korka, D., & Van Giffen, T. (2019). Digital economy report 2019. Value creation and capture: Implications for developing countries. In United Nations Conference on Trade and Development, New York.

The Economist (2019). *The AI-enabled Organisation of the Future.* London: The Economist Intelligence Unit Ltd.

4 Artificial intelligence development strategies on the global arena

Issues related to AI technology are among the most complex and the most rapidly developing concepts faced by the world and global society in the 21st century. The multi-faceted and complex nature of this phenomenon is directly affected by investments made in various areas of the economy and industry. They add considerable dynamics to both the progress as well as the scale of projects being implemented in the AI domain. On the other hand, actions taken by state governments in this regard serve two basic goals. First, to maintain and strengthen the competitiveness of the given country's economy internationally and, second, to satisfy the global consumer demand related to the continuously growing requirements and expectations of customers as well as societies for innovative goods and services. To undertake rational actions in such a turbulent organizational environment, governments must continuously monitor the situation, analyze and assess their priorities as well as design responses to any emerging challenges. In practice, state responses to such situations are expressed in national strategies for AI development (see Table 4.1), which contain long-term scenarios of goals, plans and tasks concerning AI technology implementation in different aspects of the economy and society.

4.1 United States

The United States adopted its AI strategy in 2019, calling it the **American AI Initiative**. Its main axes are actions intended to maintain the United States' leading position on the global AI market, in science, research, technology as well as innovation. These tasks should be pursued in partnership with the private sector, the scientific community and a network of research and development institutes as well as in cooperation with international stakeholders. In addition, the implementation of this initiative assumes the involvement of government authorities at all levels of the US administration. The AI Initiative is strongly focused on the implementation of five basic tasks, from the point of view of promoting AI development:[1]

- first, support and popularize long-term investment in AI research and development to contribute to creating groundbreaking (from the point of view of Humanity) technologies in all possible areas of life,

DOI: 10.4324/9781003184027-4

Table 4.1 Global readiness of national AI development strategies

Country	*Strategy name*	Years covered by *the strategy*	*Strategy preparation status*
Argentina	National Plan of Artificial Intelligence	2020-2030	pending
Australia	The Government 2025 Digital Transformation Strategy	2018-2025	pending
Austria	Artificial Intelligence Mission Austria 2030	2019–30	ready
Belgium	AI 4 Belgium	2019–30	ready
Canada	CIFAR Pan-Canadian Artificial Intelligence Strategy	2017–22	ready
China	The New Generation of Artificial Intelligence Development Plan	2017–30	ready
Colombia	National Policy for Digital Transformation i Artificial Intelligence	2019-2024	pending
Cyprus	National Strategy AI: Actions for the use and development of AI in Cyprus	n.d.	ready
Czech Republic	The National AI Strategy	2019–30	ready
Denmark	National Strategy for Artificial Intelligence	2019–27	ready
Estonia	Estonia's National AI Strategy	2019–21	ready
European Union	Communication on Artificial Intelligence	2018–27	ready
Finland	Finland's Age of Artificial Intelligence	2017–30	ready
France	Meaningful Artificial Intelligence: Towards a French and European Strategy	2018–22	ready
Germany	AI Made in Germany	2018–25	ready
Hungary	Hungary Artificial Intelligence Strategy	2020–30	ready
India	National Strategy for Artificial Intelligence	2018–30	ready
Japan	Artificial Intelligence Technology Strategy	2017–30	ready
Lithuania	Lithuanian Artificial Intelligence Strategy: A vision of the future	2019–20	ready
Luxembourg	Artificial Intelligence: A strategic strategic vision for Luxembourg	2019–30	ready
Malta	Malta the Ultimate AI Launchpad: A Strategy and Vision for Artificial Intelligence in Malta 2030	2019–30	ready
Mexico	Artificial Intelligence Strategy of Mexico 2018	2018–30	ready
The Netherlands	Dutch AI Strategy	2018–30	ready
Norway	National Strategy for Artificial Intelligence	2019-2025	ready
Poland	Artificial Intelligence Development Policy in Poland for 2019–2027	2019-2027	ready
Portugal	AI Portugal 2030	2019-2030	ready
Russia	National Strategy for the Development of Artificial Intelligence by 2030	2019-2030	ready

(*Continued*)

Table 4.1 (*Continued*)

Country	*Strategy name*	*Years covered by the strategy*	*Strategy preparation status*
Serbia	Strategy for the Development of Artificial Intelligence in the Republic of Serbia for the period 2020-2025	2020-2025	ready
Singapore	National AI Strategy	2019-2030	ready
Slovakia	Strategy of the Digital Transformation of Slovakia 2030	2019-2030	ready
South Korea	National AI Strategy to Bolster the Economy & Improve Living Standards by 2030	2019–30	ready
Spain	RDI Strategy in Artificial Intelligence	2019-2030	ready
Sweden	National approach to artificial intelligence	2019–	ready
United Arab Emirates	UAE Artificial Intelligence Strategy 2031	2019-2031	ready
United Kingdom	AI Sector Deal	2019-2030	ready
United States	The National Artificial Intelligence Research and Development Strategic Plan	2019-2030	ready
Switzerland	Digital Switzerland strategy	2018-2030	ready
Brazil	E-Digital	2018-2021	ready
Croatia Greece Ireland Israel Italy Kenya Latvia Malaysia Republic of South Africa Saudi Arabia Slovenia Tunisia Uruguay	n.d.	n.d.	pending

Source: Prepared by the authors.

- second, utilize all available resources and competences at the federal level that will foster AI development at local, federal, national as well as global levels,
- third, remove legal, regulatory, commercial, visa, customs as well as cultural barriers for innovations concerning AI,

- fourth, raise professional competences of American employees (this includes retraining of the available workforce) in the area of AI technology through training, courses, individual consultations with experts, e-learning, postgraduate studies, etc.,
- fifth, build a platform for integration, cooperation and exchange of experience in the AI sphere between the American and the international society.

An important supplement to the US AI Initiative and support for the related tasks came with the adoption, also in 2019, of the updated, national strategic plan in AI research and development 2016 (Select Committee on Artificial Intelligence of the National Science & Technology Council, 2019). It confirmed the relevance of the theses and assumptions that had been formulated with regard to researching AI a few years earlier. Simultaneously, it postulated intensification of cooperation with the private sector and increasing trust in AI through the application of a responsible and ethical approach to the solutions it offers. The update of the national strategic plan in research and development in the AI domain defined a collection of eight goals, in the form of a strategy, to strengthen the development of AI and the United States' economic position on the global innovation map. Particular strategies in this area refer to (Select Committee on Artificial Intelligence of the National Science & Technology Council, 2019):

- **strategy 1 – making long-term investments into research in AI development**. A fundamental role is to be performed by investments that will promote projects related to creating the next generation of artificial intelligence, the AI 3.0 (see Table 2.3). The projects undertaken in this sphere should provide the United States with a leading position in the global AI domain, especially since the present research that has been completed in this regard, in spite of the related high risk and costs, has already led to many spectacular achievements: the Internet, GPS localization devices, language translators, speech recognition devices, gestures, movements, medical equipment for recognizing, monitoring and analysis of disease conditions in patients, etc. Therefore, research on AI is to focus on all the aspects of human life, so that they can be beneficial in the future, in the first place for the US economy and the American society,
- **strategy 2 – developing effective person–AI cooperation methods**. This approach is to create such AI systems that will support and supplement human work. This is not about eliminating humans from the job, or replacing them directly by a machine, but directly supporting humans in those things that are repeatable, monotonous or hazardous. Owing to the fact that this scheme will increasingly dominate in many areas of life, it becomes necessary to develop appropriate methods that will foster person–machine interaction,
- **strategy 3 – identifying and understanding the consequences of AI in ethics, law and social affairs**. It is beyond doubt that AI, like any technology, creates real hazards for society, and does so in several areas.

The hazards may include loss of privacy, loss of jobs, incorrect use of personal data, emergence of new (earlier not present) medical conditions, especially in the field of psychology and psychiatry. In this context the United States' strategy in the AI sphere assumes development of a system for using AI tools to produce goods that will be consistent with the ethical, legal and social objectives of the American nation and the best interest of the United States,

- **strategy 4 – ensuring safety and protection of AI systems**. In practice, this means that all the designed AI applications must be safe, comfortable and assure trust among users. For the United States the implementation of this strategy is a great challenge, as AI systems' complexity and variability requires large financial outlays and knowledge to ensure safety in this arena. Therefore strategy 4 assumes investment in research that will increase the safety and real control over the development of AI technology in the United States,
- **strategy 5 – determining the methods of sharing public data sets for the needs of training and AI environment testing**. This strategy imposes on federal authorities the obligation to invest in the creation of public, secure data sets, which will be used for the needs of training and AI environment testing. Data collections in the United States play and will continue to play a key role from the point of view of research and development in the AI sphere, especially when it comes to speech recognition, image recognition or video surveillance applications. Currently, many such applications are utilized by the US health-care system, police and other uniformed services, including the army,
- **strategy 6 – measuring and evaluating the AI technology using specific standards and comparative tests**. This strategy defines how the developed standards and paradigms in the area of AI research and development can also be used to develop new solutions, which will be able to face the upcoming challenges. Measuring equipment, including tests, standards, experiments, is a necessary instrument used to audit and assess AI-based systems, especially in the area of their functionality as well as technical,[2] semantic[3] and process[4] interoperability,
- **strategy 7 – better understanding the domestic needs of the workforce in terms of AI research.** This strategy assumes that professional qualifications will be enhanced in order to ensure suitability of the workforce for the AI era. Currently the rapidly growing demand for specialists in the field of AI, given their shortage, forces the United States to demonstrate greater creativity in training and acquiring such employees. Simultaneously, AI experts, scientists and engineers have broad opportunities of finding a good job and of conducting research on AI development. All the actions of the United States in this area are focused on searching and acquiring AI talents who are to become the driving force in the development of this technology in the country. In addition, scientific communities in the United States are facing a growing interest of students in AI-related study majors,

- **strategy 8 – popularizing the public–private partnership, in order to accelerate AI development**. This strategy centers on promoting sustainable investment in AI research and development in the United States. Its basic elements are cooperation platforms built together by entrepreneurs, universities, international partners and state authorities for faster and more effective AI development in the United States. The strength of partnership is supposed to contribute to generation of groundbreaking AI-related technologies.

Bearing in mind the above, it is worth pointing out that the implementation of the described strategies, plans and tasks within the **AI Initiative** will require the United States to sustain, in coming years, major financial outlays on research and development related to state-of-the-art technologies. In fact, it is a necessary condition for the United States to maintain its leading position in science, artificial intelligence or quantum technology in the world in the future. Therefore, the national budget for the fiscal year 2021 includes expenditures of USD 142.2 billion on federal initiatives for promoting research and development in new technologies (OSTP, 2020). This means that, as compared to the year 2020, expenditure will increase by almost USD 9 billion. By transferring such immense funding for research and development of the **AI Initiative**, the US government wants to send a clear signal to subordinate federal agencies that they must treat AI technology as a priority. Similar status in the budget has been assigned to those sectors that are regarded as future-oriented, e.g. organizations involved in the development of quantum intelligent systems (QIS). As a result, outlays on research in this area will also increase almost twofold until 2022. In addition, the budget for 2021 assumes significant growth in investment in the area of education, training, courses and studies in fields related to AI. This financial initiative is supposed to contribute primarily to building a differentiated and highly qualified workforce in the United States, the first objective of which will be to support the development of the **Industry of the Future** across the entire country. Moreover, this project will also be supported by cooperation on the part of US higher education institutions and universities, which will receive additional funds for this purpose from the national budget.

From a synthetic perspective, between 2020 and 2022, a significant portion of the funding that the US wants to spend on the development of research in the area of innovative technologies will be shared by two concepts: one related directly to AI and the second, focused on the development of quantum intelligent systems (networks). In the case of AI, the United States budget until 2022 envisages that (OSTP, 2020):

- until 2021 there will be a significant growth in funds for R&D in the area of AI, not directly related to national defense,
- by 2022, the funds for R&D in the AI sphere, related to national defense, will have doubled,
- expenses are expected to grow for R&D in the AI sphere and for interdisciplinary research institutes within the National Science Foundation. Pursuant

to these assumptions, the United States want to transfer USD 830 million, by the end of 2021 for this purpose,

- by 2021 USD 125 million (in 2020 it was USD 71 million) will be allocated on AI research in energy,
- USD 100 million will support the Agriculture and Food Research Initiative, the aim of which is to popularize the application of AI in agricultural systems,
- USD 50 million will support the National Institute of Health, with the funds to serve them to intensify research, with the application of AI, on chronic diseases,
- by 2021 the US government agency in charge of the development of military technologies (Defense Advanced Research Projects Agency, DARPA)[5] is going to invest USD 459 million in research and development on AI. For comparison, in 2020 this amount is lower by USD 50 million.

When it comes to the second concept, development of quantum intelligent systems, the financing of this project by the United States until 2022 assumes (OSTP, 2020):

- doubling, by 2022, the expenses on investment in the field of building quantum intelligent systems,
- the National Science Foundation transferring USD 230 million by 2021 for research on QIS (in 2020 this amount was "only" USD 120 million),
- growth in government expenses for tests with regard to QIS, which in 2021 are to reach the level of USD 237 million (in 2020 this amount is smaller by nearly USD 70 million). Financial support in this area is to reach, first of all, domestic laboratories and research institutes as well as universities and industrial studios,
- transferring additional USD 25 million to support pilot research concerning the construction of the national quantum internet (QI), whose scope and potential is to exceed the classical Internet,
- annual growth in funding for research and development in areas of quantum equipment and quantum internet,
- support for the National Quantum Coordination Office, in order to standardize actions taken in the area of QIS at the federal level.

All of the above research and development activities and the scale of their funding confirm that the United States wants to be the global leader in designing network quantum devices, the more so as currently it is China that is considered a pioneer in the development of quantum communication. However, research in the area of the quantum network is very advanced around the world, the effect of which is visible in the innovative use of quantum devices to improve the operations of various economic sectors or of national security (NQCO, 2020). According to the *Strategic Vision for America's Quantum Networks*, published in February 2020 in Washington by the National Quantum Coordination Office, the long-term development potential of quantum networks in the United States will be determined by (NQCO, 2020):

- the nation's ability to build pioneer platforms that will integrate quantum devices and systems in one location,
- the nation's ability to build applications using quantum security features, sensors and advanced computational methods.

The implementation of the two actions will allow the United States to lay foundations for the domestic quantum internet. Its creation is to be guided by two goals that the US will pursue over the next two decades (NQCO, 2020):

- first, by 2025, laboratories and companies in the United States will present basic knowledge and key technologies regarding quantum networks, including quantum connections, quantum repeaters, quantum memory, high capacity quantum channels. Simultaneously, a determination will be made about the potential impact of quantum applications and systems on improving the functioning of science, medicine, industry, trade or national security,
- second, by 2040, in the United States, quantum internet connections will use quantum network devices, offering new opportunities to use the traditional Internet and better understand the role that the quantum entanglement plays in this field.

Considering the United States' strategy in quantum technology, including the funding that will be transferred in coming years for its development, it is impossible not to have an impression that this nation aspires to play the leader's role in the second quantum revolution presently happening across the world. To a significant extent, it is caused by the potential and the opportunities offered by the technology being described here, which makes it possible to solve complex problems that even the greatest supercomputers in the world would not cope with. In addition, thanks to the integration of quantum technology and AI in the future it will be possible to predict its development more precisely. In practice, long-term forecasts, not only economic ones, will be characterized by both higher accuracy and precision of measurements and calculations. Benefits for countries that arise from the application of and the development of quantum technology, have led the United States into strong competition with China, aimed at achieving global competitive advantage in this domain.[6] While there are a lot of voices from many groups now, definitely claiming that China has already surpassed the United States in key quantum technology-related elements and concepts, right now the supremacy of both China and the United States in this area cannot be undermined. Only the EU (the fifth economy in the world) is an entity that in the near future may join the group of world quantum technology leaders, which will be addressed further in this chapter, discussing in more detail the problems of AI strategies also in the context of the EU (see section 4.3).

4.2 China

China, alongside the United States and governments of other forward-thinking countries, believes that the development of AI will be the key strategy which will determine national competitive advantage over the next several decades. Furthermore, I. Gill (2020) from Duke University states that: "who introduces artificial intelligence by the year 2030 will rule the world until 2100", that is for the next seven decades. China, next to the United States, undoubtedly also aspires to the group of world leaders in this area, already implementing basic technologies, procedures and standards in AI-related fields. And while Chinese authorities are strongly competing for the role of world leader in groundbreaking technologies of general application, they also effectively protect their prior achievements and discoveries in the AI domain, especially those related directly to national security. Thus, it is beyond doubt that this country's authorities are fully aware of the power and the driving force that AI technology will become in the future for areas of the economy related to production, distribution, consumption, logistics, and to defense as well as the areas related to social aspects of life, concerning interpersonal relations, social bonds, lifestyles, thinking and communication or the holistic culture system. Thus, China wants to make use of AI potential to build the welfare state and maintain long-term macroeconomic stability of the economy. Apart from that, AI technology is also to become a special panacea for the socio-economic problems faced by this country in recent years, including:

- **the aging society** – the restrictive birth control policy implemented in the years 1977–2015 has led to a situation in which, according to the National Working Commission for China Ageing, the number of people aged 60 and more will increase until 2050 in China to 487 million, which will account for nearly 35 percent of the entire population,[7]
- **pollution of the natural environment** – at present, China is the largest CO_2 emitter in Asia and the world, responsible for more than 25 percent of the global CO_2 emissions,
- **education and higher education** – since 2010 the Chinese government has been pursuing a 10-year plan for the reform and development of medium- and long-term education. The initiative aims to contribute to eliminating problems that have grown in the Chinese education system since 1991,[8] which primarily include (Cai, 2013): a surge in the number of students, with insufficient infrastructural, HR and financial resources, low level of education, lack of innovation in education processes, development of a homogeneous higher education structure not matching the needs of the labor market and not serving the national economy as a whole, equal access to education both at the regional level (city–country), and the social level (the poor–the rich),
- **economic stratification of society** – rapid economic growth during last three decades[9] has created a situation in which the gap between the rich and the poor Chinese citizens has widened. As a result, according to the ranking Gini Coefficient by Country 2020 – World Population Review,[10] the Gini

coefficient for China reached 0.465 in 2019. For comparison, in the United States, Germany or Switzerland it was respectively: 0.450, 0.270 and 0.295.[11]

Owing to the fact that AI technology has the potential to increase current levels of precision, complexity or customization, both when it comes to the creation of goods, provision of services or improvement in the quality of life, it should be expected that proper management of AI development will bring measurable benefits both to China and other nations, the more so in that China has stable foundations for AI development, both in economic, social, cultural, geopolitical or scientific terms. These foundations were laid some time ago, when the national authorities started the implementation process of innovative projects and investing large funds in scientific research (see Figure 4.1). As a result, governmental projects were substantially expanded and strengthened, focusing, for example, on the development of smart manufacturing, which later marked the beginning of smart factories. With their formation, machines working in Chinese enterprises started to exchange information with other production equipment, and middle and senior management gained information necessary to make critical decisions.

In addition, effective actions have been taken with regard to promoting initiatives concerning the creation of e-commerce ecosystems or smart transmission grids. In the case of the latter, it is worth mentioning that China already operates monumental ultra-high voltage transmission lines (UHVDC), which, thanks to

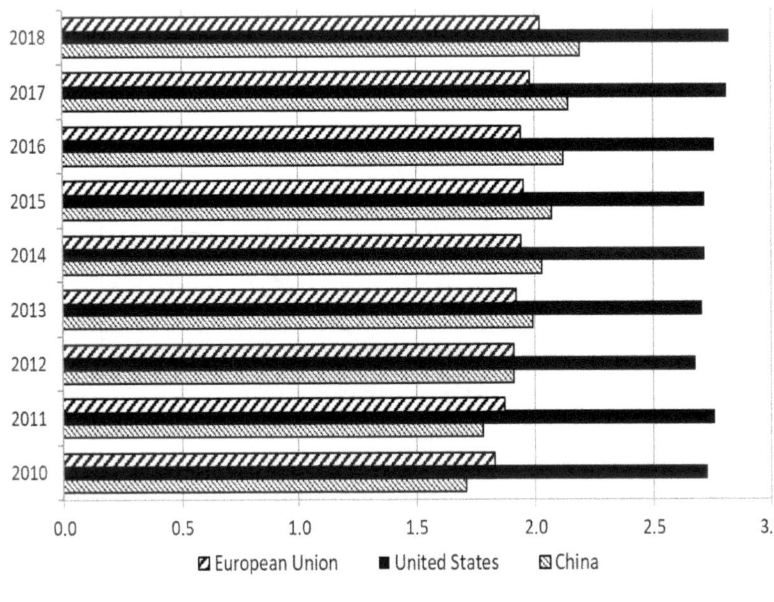

Figure 4.1 Expenditure of the European Union, the United States and China on research and development in the period 2010–2018 (as % of GDP). Source: Prepared by the authors on the basis of the data from OECD Science, Technology and R&D Statistics: Main Science and Technology Indicators.

modern solutions, transfer wind and water energy collected in various parts of the country to Chinese cities and metropolises. In addition, China can also boast of significant accomplishments in AI technology development in the scientific field, confirmed by the fact that for over 20 years this country has been ranked second in the world, just after the United States, in the number of published scientific articles regarding artificial intelligence. However, if we take into account the number of patents held by China, not only in the AI field, but in general, it turns out that (see Figure 4.2) the country has been the world leader since 2011. As an example, as early as 2018 it had nearly 950,000 patents more than the United States (see Figure 4.2).

Although AI technology is used on a large scale and the plans concerning its development are very ambitious,[12] the country's authorities are still facing many challenges, mostly related to limiting or totally eliminating the gaps growing in the country, primarily regarding the level of pay, competences, development or legal issues. These tasks will require Chinese authorities to undertake initiatives that will give the correct long-term direction to the development of AI technology in this country. They are to be based on the AI strategy adopted by the State Council of the People's Republic of China in July 2017, which is a kind of road map for building China's global competitive advantage in the AI domain. The AI strategy "A New Generation of Artificial Intelligence Development Plan" (The State Council of China, 2017), presents long-term goals, which China will pursue until 2030 in the context of this country's determination to become the world leader in the AI domain. In the opinion of Chinese authorities, this huge project will require far-reaching activities in many areas of economic, social and

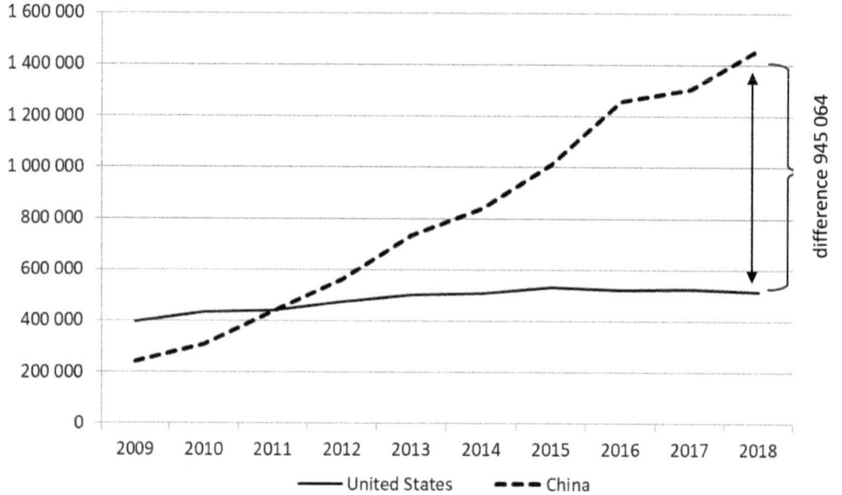

Figure 4.2 Number of patents held by the United States and China in the years 2009–2018. Source: Own study based on WIPO statistics database.

cultural life (The State Council of China, 2017). First, they center on dynamic initiatives for building an intelligent market economy, smart factories and smart cities. Notable support for the implementation of this idea will come from the creation and then merging of network ecosystems with business clusters to create a platform for the integration of knowledge, technologies, ideas, talents, but also challenges and threats related to AI technology. This solution will increase both manufacturing and social strength and potential of the Chinese nation in designing an innovative country and a scientific and technical global power. Second, a key task for Chinese authorities will be to support financially those entrepreneurs and enterprises whose achievements will prove groundbreaking from the perspective of increasing the potential of primary AIs. Third, the Chinese authorities are clear, that in pursuit of global leadership in the AI domain they also want to take advantage of the socialist system, in the form of opportunities that each citizen will get if they are involved in actions intended to build together the innovative capabilities of the Chinese economy. Fourth, the government will strongly support actions intended to promote knowledge, research and innovations as well as sharing their results with other market participants. Moreover, new patterns of military and civil integration in science and research will be developed. The Chinese authorities also assure that the country will pursue active participation in global AI research, development and management, all the while caring for the global optimization of innovative resource allocation (The State Council of China, 2017). And fifth, a direct measure of the Chinese nation's achievements in AI field will be the scale of the commercial application of technological innovations in this field, in various areas of China's social and economic life.

According to the AI strategy adopted in China, the implementation of its strategic goals has been divided into three stages (The State Council of China, 2017):

- **stage I** – are the objectives to be implemented **by 2020**. In a synthetic perspective, they are to focus on supporting AI application in the country's economy on an advanced, global level, since Industry 4.0 in general and AI in particular are today perceived as key factors of economic growth. Furthermore, AI technology itself is today identified as the main tool that determines improvement in living conditions of individuals and forms of support for many industries. Therefore, large-scale data processing, smart machines, intelligent autonomous systems, smart monitoring systems and parameter processing are just selected areas where significant progress has occurred and groundbreaking results have often been achieved. In this context, the Chinese authorities are aware of the fast growth in competitiveness of AI technology not only internationally, but also globally. Therefore, they want to support financially entrepreneurs and industries related to this area, with CNY 1 trillion.[13] In addition, the labor market is to be stimulated to promote search and collection of data about highly qualified AI specialists. The state will also aim to regulate legal problems related to the ethical aspects of using AI technology-based solutions,

- **stage II** – are the objectives to be implemented **by 2025**. By that time, China plans to have achieved significant progress in AI, allowing them to be perceived as the global leader in this field. In the opinion of the Chinese authorities, to achieve this status AI technology must become the fundamental driving force of modernization and transformation of the Chinese economy. Only then can the pursuit of building an intelligent industry and an innovative economy be realized. China also wants to be a pioneer in building a new generation of AI technology, which will contribute to groundbreaking discoveries in many areas of life related to manufacturing, transportation, medical care, life in cities, agriculture, safety, etc. According to the information contained in the strategy, the value of the Chinese AI industry may reach as much as CNY 400 billion or more.[14] Caring about the safety and control over AI, the Chinese authorities plan to prepare and adopt respective legal policies to secure their interests and those of the whole society,
- **stage III** – are the objectives to be implemented **by 2030**. By that date, China's aspiration is to become the most important center of worldwide innovation in the AI domain. This will allow the authorities and society to reach the innovative and highly developed country status and will be possible thanks to groundbreaking discoveries in human brain intelligence, collective intelligence, mixed intelligence or analytical intelligence. China will thus aim at constant AI development in industry, manufacturing, social life, transport or construction, where a significant support element will be the AI platforms and business ecosystems created on a large scale. In addition, their ambition is to create a training base at the global level, which will "forge" experts in various AI knowledge areas.

Bearing in mind the above and that the primary goal of Chinese authorities is to make China the main AI innovation center of the world, the AI strategy in this country has been additionally supported by six actions. They are related to (He, 2017):

- **creation of the legal, regulatory and ethical framework** – this applies e.g. to conducting scientific research that will define the scope of civil and penal liability concerning e.g. property and privacy protection of both individuals and legal entities in activities related to the application of AI. Therefore, it is vital to define the rights, obligations and the scope of responsibility of each AI entity. In addition, it is necessary to prepare detailed regulatory provisions, especially in these areas, where AI technology is already applied, or is to be applied in the near future. Similar actions, including also on the research arena, will be required by issues relating to the ethical and moral aspects of the human–machine cooperation. Therefore, the initiative of the Chinese authorities aiming to develop an ethical code of conduct for all AI stakeholders should be considered a step in the right direction. This project is in a way a confirmation that China wants to actively participate in managing AI development not only on the international, but above all the global scale,

- **implementation of policies stimulating faster AI development** – this action is to be achieved by the policy of tax incentives for small, middle and large enterprises. Additionally, the authorities' support in this field can be beneficial for these entities that will implement pilot projects based on innovative ideas employing highly advanced digital technology,
- **development of AI technology and intellectual property standards** – this task is concerned with establishing and verifying technical, professional or evaluation standards for all AI-related entities. These standards should be developed both at the national and the international level, in order to ensure that they can serve a group of stakeholders at the global level. In addition, a particularly urgent case is to strengthen the current regulations regarding intellectual property protection, especially with regard to AI technology. The protection of patents and codification of AI-based solutions must serve the development of this technology in new products and services, not yet commercialized,
- **building a safe system of AI regulations, assessments and protection** – this action relates not only to enhancing research on the impact of AI on national security, but also to the creation of the mechanisms for continuous monitoring of safe AI development. Such an approach is to support the design of a map of risks and limitations that at every stage accompany the development of innovative technologies, including AI. Therefore, the creation of transparent regulations concerning the development and functioning of this concept will be conducive to its easier supervision and control,
- **employment, including increasing the number of training programs for the workforce** – the essence of this project is the need to take prompt actions, intended to satisfy the growing needs of the labor market for highly-qualified AI specialists. One of the methods of dealing with such problems is the construction of a learning and training system, which will be able to deliver appropriate employees to the labor market. The pillars of such an educational system should be universities, vocational schools, scientific institutes and private training companies, organizations or enterprises. Due to such a strategy, employees' professional skills will increase, and highly qualified work posts will be filled,
- **creating awareness of activities related to scientific AI education** – this action, synthetically, is concerned with the process of educating society about AI technology and its forming elements. It can be pursued by employees' participation in events (workshops, conferences, symposiums, scientific meetings, congresses) devoted to the AI sphere. An important form of support for this type of initiative is also the creation and implementation of domestic AI-related educational programs, which can also be transferred as curricula to primary and middle schools. Another important element conducive to the popularization of any science is also the creation of science or innovation centers, where visitors have the opportunity to witness practical AI applications in everyday life.

By defining the AI strategy, including a number of actions necessary for it to materialize, the Chinese authorities have made a significant step towards becoming a country of global-level innovation and the leading economy in the near future.

4.3 European Union

The recent worldwide development of AI, including in the EU, has been unique in terms of magnitude. As a result, many Europeans already today use the facilities or, synthetically speaking, life improvements that are offered by this technology, e.g. they are better and faster diagnosed for diseases, their work is becoming more efficient with modern applications, and the decisions they make as business owners are, as a result of using predictive analysis, more relevant and thereby bearing a smaller risk. However, next to the benefits which AI delivers, there are also a number of potential hazards. They apply both to people's social sphere and their private or emotional one, as illustrated by elderly people's fear of digital exclusion. In order to maximize the benefits and minimize the risks involved in AI, the EU must operate as a single entity on further prospects of its development and the implementation of AI solutions into the daily life of European citizens. In fact, only such an approach offers guarantees that the common purpose of transnational use of new technologies to improve the material, social and professional status of each European can be achieved, with simultaneous respect for any rights vested therein. Bearing this in mind, in February 2020, the European Commission (EC) published its White Paper[15] on Artificial Intelligence, which presents the European AI development strategy and the related approach to data management. The White Paper[16] defines the strategic goals which must be undertaken within EU structures, to allow the Union to become, just as the United States and China, a global leader in the area of innovative AI-based solutions. An important role in pursuing this strategic goal is to be served by all EU Member States and EU institutions as well as representatives of industry, social and civic organizations, the world of science and other stakeholders, all keenly interested in cooperation and partnership for the development of the European AI strategy.

Considering the White Paper and the approach to further development of the AI technology, algorithms or computational power in Europe it presents, the EU representatives are proposing the creation and expansion of an AI ecosystem within the EU. It is to serve for the collection of expert knowledge on AI, which will later materialize in AI products and services, and thus provide economic and social benefits for the whole EU community in three key areas related to (European Commission, 2020):

- **citizen interests** – in this case, the focus is to enable access to better medical care, manufacture daily-use devices that will be less prone to failure and whose repair will also be possible remotely, enable access to safer and less carbon-intensive means of transport, a greater selection of e-work offers on the market, the possibility to obtain more precise forecasts, reports, simulations regarding trends in the economy, industry, agriculture, services, science, society, etc.,

- **enterprise interests** – the point is to ensure their long-term, stable development, especially in such sectors of the economy where they play a leading role in the global arena and demonstrate high potential from the perspective of creating new AI-based solutions. In this context, within the EU, particularly strong are companies from the sectors: machine, automotive, fuel, petrochemical, financial, energy or tourism.[17] In the case of the latter, the EU authorities will aim, under innovative AI technology solutions, to keep Europe as the most popular tourist location worldwide,
- **public interest** – which will take into account the objectified needs of the entire European society, related to e.g. living cost reduction, improvement in remote access to institutions and state offices, improvement in public (or more broadly: national) safety by use of smart monitoring and supervision tools, respect for civil rights and liberties (privacy protection).

Apart from announcing the creation of the European AI ecosystem, the White Paper also includes a description of the strategic variants that are to guarantee the creation of artificial intelligence that is safe and trustworthy throughout Europe. In practice, there are two variants and they have been defined from the political as well as regulatory perspective, where (European Commission, 2020):

- **the political perspective** – assumes that it is necessary to define measures that are to support the merging of the efforts both at the EU, national, regional as well as local level in order to fulfill the established aspirations in the AI area. One of the responses to this type of initiative is to create an **ecosystem of excellence** in Europe. In practice, this approach assumes the concentration on those things, industries, sectors or values, that make the EU strong internationally. In other words, in its approach to AI, the point is not that the EU "blindly" imitate China or the United States, but does what is close to it, similar to it and natural for it. The strength of this solution, which is also to be implemented in the form of public–private partnerships, lies in the EU's diversity. In fact, the strength of the EU's economy is based on it being formed by enterprises that come from different Member States, have different sizes and production scales, are recognizable in their industries on the markets all over the world, and create consortia under EU programs for implementation of common business goals that are often global in nature. In this context, the European cooperation paradigm consisting in a combination of diversity and experience with innovation creates even greater chances of discovering new ideas, products or services related to AI technology. It is important as the largest companies in the world come, first of all from the United States[18] and, in smaller numbers, from China, Japan, South Korea or Singapore, and such companies have easier access to data or large computational powers than smaller ones. This does not imply that the EU is at a disadvantage in this "race". The point is only that, competing with the world economic powers, it utilizes its strength – namely diversity and the ability to engage in multi-dimensional cooperation,

- **regulatory perspective** – assumes that a key role in the future from the point of view of AI development in Europe will be played by the developed and then implemented legal regulations. In the opinion of the EC representatives, they will create the **ecosystem of trust**, namely a plane (regulatory system) to promote trust and clarity among the stakeholders, including in their approach to AI in business. At the end of the day, this solution will have an impact on building a sustainable economy as well as a sustainable society. Building in society a climate of trust for a new concept or technology is always conducive to promoting cooperation, increased engagement and motivation to work among the citizens, strengthened bonds, improved effectiveness, increase in the number of ideas and creative solving of problems and emergencies. In practice, the functioning of the ecosystem of trust is to ensure respect for the regulations and provisions existing within the EU and concerning, e.g. protection of citizens' (consumers') fundamental rights, in particular with reference to AI-based applications or solutions used in daily life by Europeans, intellectual property and copyright protection, privacy and personal data protection. Therefore, the initiative taken up by the EC for building the ecosystem of trust is to encourage EU citizens to "boldly" apply and utilize AI in practice, and entrepreneurs to initiate projects in the AI arena, which, when materialized, will serve the entire European society. Therefore, the EC will firmly support the approach (European Commission, 2020): "the center of which is the human being and which will be based on the message regarding the building of human-concentrated trust in AI".

The foundation of implementing strategic AI development options in the EU is the creation of two ecosystems: of excellence and of trust. This idea will require extensive cooperation and several key actions, especially from representatives of EU authorities. When it comes to the **ecosystem of excellence**, its construction will require (European Commission, 2020):

- **declared cooperation with Member States of the EU** – this action aims for:
  a) by 2027 the implementation of nearly 70 common activities improving the effectiveness of cooperation between EU Member States and the European Commission, in such areas as scientific research, investment, international cooperation, competences and skills, data management,
  b) between 2020–30 increasing financial outlays on investment in AI, by over EUR 20 billion,

c) launching the **Digital Europe**[19] Program in 2021, to provide financial support for the digital transformation of the EU national economies and their societies,
d) the implementation, between 2021–27, of the EU framework program in scientific research and innovation entitled **Horizon Europe**[20] with the aim to strengthen both the EU's scientific and technological foundation and the European potential in the area of innovation,
e) launching, under a new financial perspective for the period 2021–27, European structural and investment funds consolidating AI development in the EU,
f) promotion of solutions with regard to AI, which will foster elimination and mitigation of climate changes and natural environment degradation, improved utilization of scarce natural resources and electric energy, increased social welfare.

- **focusing on the actions of the scientific and research environment and innovation pioneers on the right path** – as part of this action the following is intended:
  a) building a network of research and scientific centers that will be involved in broadening the area of knowledge in the field of AI and coordination of their activities in order to achieve the synergy effect in joint research on the practical application of AI in everyday life,
  b) building a flagship AI scientific research, innovation and knowledge center that will serve as the coordinator in the development of AI in Europe, and use its authority to attract investment and best talent in the AI domain,
  c) building experimental centers – in sectors where the EU can become the global leader, in order to support the development and introduction of new AI applications into the life of organizations and societies.

- **development of skills** – as part of this action the following are intended:
  a) launching the European program for the development of skills, the aim of which is to supplement the emerging shortage of competences in EU Member States, especially in the AI field,
  b) continuous updates of the action plan in digital education, in order to adjust education systems and training to the needs of the digital economy,
  c) revision of the workforce's qualifications in EU Member States in order to speedily adapt it to AI-related transformation,
  d) activation of women who, thanks to their qualifications, can find employment in the AI sector.

- **focusing the actions of small and medium enterprises** – within this action the following are intended:
  a) ensuring access for small and medium enterprises (SME) to AI technology and the opportunities of using the solutions it offers,

b) creating at least one innovation center in each member country, which will have a high degree of specialization in the AI domain,
c) launching in the 1st quarter 2020, by the European Commission and the European Investment Fund[21] (EIF), a pilot program, the aim of which is to ensure capital financing[22] for the development of AI and blockchain.

- **building a partnership with the private sector** – as part of this action the following are intended:
  a) development of public–private partnership in the domains of AI, data and robotics, in order to ensure the development of scientific research and innovation in these areas and the required level of co-investment within the EU.

- **promoting the use of AI by the public sector** – within this action the following are intended:
  a) popularization of AI technology among public administration institutions and offices,
  b) conducting a series of sector dialogues which are to contribute to the emergence of a special program for the implementation of AI in the processes, systems, regulations and work of the public administration.

- **provision of access to data and the computational infrastructure** – within this action the following are intended:
  a) improvement in access to data and their management, in order to ensure their optimal and more effective utilization for the benefit of the society and the development of AI in the EU,
  b) growth in financial outlays – to more than EUR 4 billion – on the development of key computational and quantum technologies within the EU,
  c) accomplishment of all the tasks envisaged in the European Data Strategy which are to build a **single data market**[23] and develop the digital future of Europe.

- **taking initiatives on the international level** – as part of this action the following are intended:
  a) development of the ethical principles in the AI domain in cooperation with OECD and G-20 group,[24]
  b) cooperation in global AI development with the Council of Europe, UNESCO, OECD, WTO[25] or ITU,[26]
  c) global monitoring of AI development strategies in other countries around the world.

In the case of the **ecosystem of trust**, its construction will be focused on (European Commission, 2020):

- a **clear definition of the problem** – under this action the following is proposed:
  a) determination of both tangible and intangible damage which can be caused by AI along with the estimated levels of related risk,

b) preparation of the legal regulations to counteract problems related to technological errors (defects) created at the implementation stages of AI projects.

- **adaptation, when necessary, of the EU's existing legal framework in the AI domain** – as part of this action the following is proposed:
  a) preparation of regulations regarding e.g. security, liability for manufactured products and services, consumer protection, employment, racial equality, rights of women and men or personal data that will be adapted to the newly created AI products and services.

- **determination of the scope of application of the EU's future legal regulations in the AI sphere** – as part of this action the following are proposed:
  a) updates to current EU regulations regarding AI, that will reflect the digital transformation and AI application in the EU,
  b) preparation and adoption of an approach based on risk analysis with reference to the application of the proportionality of the AI regulatory intervention in the area of the market and all entities operating on it,
  c) determination of the criteria that will assess the relation between risk and the consequences of practical AI application.

- **definition of the legal requirements concerning AI imposed on entities** – as part of this action the following is proposed:
  a) a detailed specification of the legal standards imposed on entities utilizing high-risk AI in order to apply proper proportionality of the regulatory intervention.

- **division of the legal obligations between the entities concerned and geographic determination of legislative intervention** – this action proposes:
  a) settlement of the legal obligations resulting from the application of AI in the way that each of such obligations would be directed to an entity or entities that could best identify any kinds of hazards in the field of their operations,
  b) consultation concerning determination of the geographic scope of the legislative intervention with regard to business entities that manufacture AI-based goods, on EU territory.

- **determination of the principles and ways to enforce adopted law in the AI domain** – as part of this action the following is proposed:
  a) consultations within EU Member States and then preparation and implementation of a system based on conformity assessments. This system will serve the EU authorities (competent authorities, established for this

purpose) to examine individual cases related to AI-utilizing entities' compliance with the principles of safety, trust, values and laws binding on the territory of the EU.

- **voluntary labeling of AI applications not characterized by a high level of risk** – this action proposes:
  a) establishment of a new legal instrument that would define the framework for voluntary labeling by entities of those AI solutions that are not characterized by high risk. In other words, the point is to create a kind of a "quality mark" for the goods manufactured on the basis of AI, which would inform users that the product or service is safe and trustworthy from the point of view of AI.

- **proper management and oversight** – this action assumes:
  a) creation of the European Governance Structure on AI, in the form of the cooperation framework at the level of the EU Member States, in order to observe accountability, increase EU possibilities within the supervision over AI and building a plane for necessary testing and certification of AI-based goods.

The proposals presented above, contained within the White Paper, are actions, not being essentially legal acts, which within the nearest decade are to allow the EU to compete with the United States and China for global leadership in the AI domain. The EU plans to spend more than EUR 200 billion in total for this purpose until 2030. Owing to the fact that it is difficult to forecast exactly how AI technology will affect humanity and society, the European Commission has decided to lay down its framework on the principle of excellence and trust. This solution is to foster the creation of a climate not only of loyalty, but first of all safety in EU citizens' approach to AI-based solutions. Public consultations on the White Paper were, in the opinion of the European Commission, to end on 19 May 2020.

4.4 Brazil

Brazil is one of the few countries (see Table 4.1), which has had a ready strategy for the development of the digital economy and AI. It was prepared in 2018, entirely under the auspices of the Brazilian Ministry of Science, Technology, Innovation and Communication (MCTIC). Created on the initiative of the government, the document in practice reflects the commitment of all its parties, including the private sector, the public sector, academic community, civic associations and organizations or ordinary citizens, to building a national plan for the development of the digital economy in Brazil. The content of the strategy itself was filled with a description of the tools, methods, techniques and goals that, if applied and accomplished, are to contribute to deep socio-economic transformations of Brazilian society on the way to the development of the e-economy and improved quality of life. Importantly, the strategy also clearly emphasizes, many times, that all Brazilians must be the subject, and not an object of these changes. In other words, each of them must have their own share, and the adopted solutions cannot deprive anybody of equal opportunities in access to the potential offered by the digital or quantum technologies. Apart from that, Brazil, just like China, United States or the EU, wants to take advantage internationally of its competences and the technological knowledge (know-how) it possesses and become an active actor in the transformations and build global leadership in these areas, where the country is regarded as strong and competent (e.g. possible AI applications in agribusiness). An important element of the strategy is also the challenge of completing by 2030 the tasks set before Brazil by the United Nations (UN) within the Sustainable Development Goals[27] framework, which relate to ending poverty and hunger, improvementsin the level of health and quality of life, increasing levels of education, development of knowledge, innovation and online infrastructure as well as limiting pollution of the natural environment.

The Brazilian digital technology development strategy has been built to provide an integrated approach to digitization, AI, robotics, etc., as a result of assigning specific tasks to be performed by key actors, i.e. the public and private sector. Importantly, their performance, at every stage, is subject to verification by applying appropriate indicators measuring the effectiveness and the efficiency of the actions. Graphically (see Figure 4.3), both the relations between the two parties and actions the performance of which is to support the construction of the digital economy, complement and penetrate each other, at the same time creating two axes of reference, one of which is concerned with transformation, the other one with enabling actions. As regards the enabling actions (enablers), their role comes down to the creation of an environment that will foster transformation

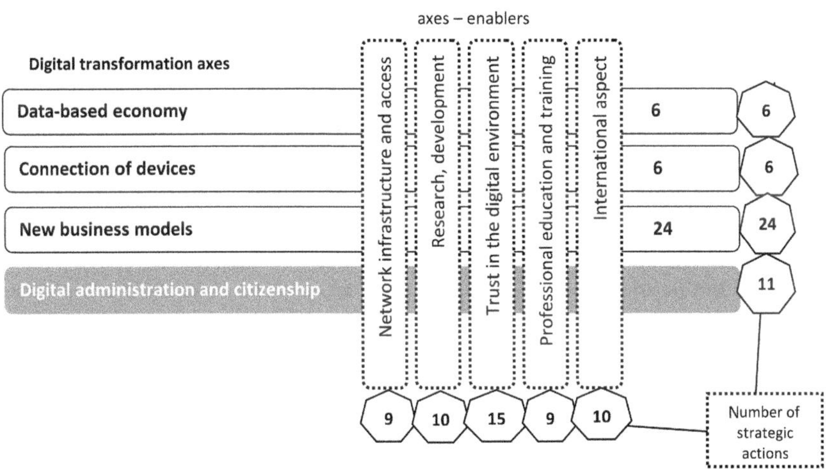

Figure 4.3 Brazil's digital economic transformation environment – the system of transformers and enablers. Source: Own study based on MCTIC (2018).

of the Brazilian economy (MCTIC, 2018). Therefore, in the opinion of MCTIC (2018), initiatives should be taken with an aim to:

- build a proper infrastructure which will allow for access to advanced ICT and communication technologies,
- develop and intensify activities in testing and creation of innovative products and services,
- develop a regulatory environment the principles of which will be respected and will have the trust of stakeholders,
- improve educational skills and professional qualifications that will be key from the perspective of developing AI technology or quantum technology,
- ensure Brazil's presence in the international environment, which will shape and set the goals in developing the global digital economy.

In this way the systematic emergence of enabling actions is to simultaneously foster the performance of transformation actions in the Brazilian economy in the form of the development of the data-driven economy, integration of systems and devices, creation of innovative business models (new models of organization management) and deepening of the digitization level of the Brazilian public administration and Brazilian society. Each of the thematic axes presented in Figure 4.3 contains a number of strategic activities which, if implemented, are to support the construction of a new digital economy based on AI technology. In the case of the **enablers** axis, they are connected with areas related to (MCTIC, 2018):

a) **infrastructure and access to information and communication technologies**. Owing to the fact that the telecommunications sector has become the main driving force in the world's socio-economic development, the authorities in Brazil want to pursue fast growth of Internet access for all Brazilians as well as to new digital technologies. However, the fulfillment of this task will require implementation of mechanisms for pursuing the following priorities:
    - connection of 22 000 public schools (municipal and rural) with fast broadband Internet under the national program Connected Education,
    - acquisition of funds for construction of broadband networks,
    - acquisition of funds for the construction of mobile broadband networks,
    - acceleration of implementation of the 4G network, operating in 700 MHz band,
    - introduction of tax reliefs at the level of the state (regional) administration, in order to promote projects to extend the range of mobile networks in areas outside cities,
    - adjustment of the regulatory provisions in the area of telecommunications to actions related to expansion of broadband networks,
    - activation of Brazilian scientific institutes in preparing international standards and norms for 5th generation cellular telephony (5G),
    - integration of scientific, research, educational and training facilities for the purpose of implementing the Giga[28] project, which assumes use and

implementation of optical network technologies in various sectors of the Brazilian economy,
- implementation of long-term investment in ICT, in particular in critical infrastructure.[29]

b) **development of research and innovation**. Brazil's investment in research, development and innovation (R+D+I) are to become the driving force for improvement in the quality of socio-economic life. The key role in this area is to be played by new technological knowledge from IT and communication technology development which is to serve also, perhaps first of all, those areas of the country that are least developed. As before, the fulfillment of this task will require implementation of mechanisms for pursuing the following priorities:
- construction, as part of national security and defense, of platforms that ensure interoperability and cooperation of all types of Brazil's armed forces along with the need for the private sector to become involved in these actions,
- introduction of electronic circulation of documents in the Brazilian health-care system by purchasing proper data communication infrastructure, which simultaneously is to provide the basis for the development of telemedicine in this country,
- digitization of agribusiness by purchasing technologies related to precise agriculture, unmanned aircraft, remote sensing or database management in agriculture,
- the development of IoT, which should be broadly applied in the context of creating smart cities, smart transmission grids, intelligent water and sewage grid management systems, intelligent CCTV systems, etc.,
- construction of research facilities and scientific institutes devoted to the development of AI technology, in order to ensure a strategic approach to the development of the data-driven economy,
- preparation of long-term scenarios in the field of research, development and innovation that in the future will contribute to a higher employment rate, citizens' income, productivity and the level of competitiveness of Brazil's economy,
- improvement of the Brazilian legislative and regulatory framework in the field of research, development and innovation, in order to increase their quality, transparency, credibility and predictability,
- launching scholarship programs (such as e.g. RHAE[30]) as support tools for the development of the research and innovation sector,
- building a permanent dialogue forum between the government, the academic environment, and industry, in order to implement the e-economy development strategy,
- extension of the scientific and technology partnerships on the international level, in order to increase the number of joint scientific projects,
- strengthening government scientific institutes at the level of research, experience and communication,
- financial support for R&D projects in new digital technologies.

c) **building trust and certainty in the digital environment**. The authorities in Brazil will not cease their efforts to build an Internet environment that will be safe for all users and that will respect the rights, but also obligations, related to personal data protection, privacy protection or protection of copyright and intellectual rights of all its stakeholders. Such an approach, especially in the age of a surge in business, financial and operating transactions, seems to be worth imitation in the opinion of the Brazilian authorities. Therefore, the fulfillment of this task will require implementation of mechanisms for pursuing the following priorities:
   - adoption of a new law on personal data protection,
   - creation of mechanisms of cooperation between public institutions and labor market organizations, in order to protect basic human rights online,
   - strengthening cooperation at the international level to ensure the application of and respect for legal regulations in the digital environment,
   - designation of a national authority, along with specification of its competences, to be competent in the field of personal data protection and international data flow,
   - preparation and definition of security regulations, norms, standards and certificates in the area of consumer data protection,
   - construction of new management models for data being the property of citizens.

d) **education and professional qualifications**. Advanced and innovative technologies will revolutionize the Brazilian labor market. This means that, as a result of the development of digital technologies and e-economy, a significant number of the present professions will either be remodeled, or totally eliminated. Instead of them, new, previously unknown ones will appear. The newly created professions will predominantly require innovative abilities to cope with technologically advanced devices, systems or machines based on AI. In this context, digital education, which puts emphasis on permanent raising of the professional qualifications and acquisition of meta-skills, becomes an important challenge for the implementation of Brazil's adopted social and economic development strategy. Bearing this in mind, the implementation of the task related to raising professional qualifications and education will require implementation of mechanisms for pursuing the following priorities:
   - implementation, at the level of secondary education, of a program developing high school students' competences in the sphere of computational systems and data analysis,
   - preparation of a new educational policy at the national level that will take account of the technological infrastructure, remote teaching as well as digital education resources as a fundamental element of the teaching process,
   - developing a new financing model for fast Internet for the Brazilian public education system,
   - development of a system for improving teachers' professional qualifications in the field of e-education and promotion of digital content that will be developed by them for the purpose of the educational process,

- preparation of a scenario concerning the possibility of replacing analog educational resources with digital media in the primary education and higher education system,
- assigning priority to such subjects as mathematics, statistics, analysis or engineering in educating society (women and men), preparing it for the challenges related to the development of the digital economy,
- development of a training system that, thanks to certification, will increase the level of professional skills related to digital technologies. It is important that such initiatives be carried out in cooperation with other partners, enterprises or organizations.

e) **the international dimension**. The main objective of this task is to strengthen the Brazilian leadership internationally in the area of digital technologies, AI and robotics. On this forum an important role is to be played by, first of all, Brazilian companies and research and development centers. It is their commitment that will reflect Brazil's determination to create the digital economy and improve the quality of life of its citizens. The fulfillment of this task will require implementation of mechanisms for pursuing the following priorities:
   - participation in international forums devoted to security online, digital security, legal regulations related to AI technology, solving conflicts in the cyber-environment, etc. along with taking advantage of partnerships in those and other areas, with the EU, MERCOSUR,[31] BRICS,[32] G20 or UN,
   - connecting Brazilian enterprises to the international data communication and electronic market segment,
   - development of international cooperation in order to promote Brazilian products and services on the global Internet,
   - promotion of the Brazilian SME sector and the goods it manufactures on international markets.

   Apart from the above actions, forming part of the enablers axis, the Brazilian digital environment and AI development strategy contain two final tasks that MCTIC representatives (2018) assigned to the digital transformation axis (see Figure 4.3). In practice, they relate to:

f) **digital transformation in the economy**. In fact, this task of the Brazilian authorities is to focus on the stimulation of actions conducive to the development of the digital and productive economy, which is to be capable of competing with the most developed countries worldwide. It means the need to improve human activities, production processes and the level of performance in all sectors of the Brazilian economy. The key element in this transformation will be data resources, the quality of which, along with the processing ability, will determine the country's competitive advantage. The digitization of the Brazilian economy will require the authorities to take a lot of actions, the most important being those related to (MCTIC, 2018):
   - promotion of foreign investments in Brazil, especially in the area of data management,

- promotion of international cooperation in the field of regulations and harmonization of regulations related to data,
- promotion of cooperation between the government, universities and the private sector, in order to exchange knowledge, experiences and technologies related to data management,
- development of a policy encouraging the use of the computational cloud in public administration,
- preparation of scenarios regarding the potential effect of digital technologies, AI, large data resources or quantum technology on social and economic growth in Brazil, subject to the opportunities, possibilities, hazards and challenges that these technologies bring along for the Brazilian society,
- approval of the national IoT development plan in Brazil,
- improvement of the legal framework related to cooperation of the enterprises' sector with scientific and research centers, in order to implement more projects for the development of the digital economy,
- conducting a lot of consultations on the ethical aspects of using algorithms in automaton of the decision-making process,
- improvement of the legal framework related to the labor market and the workforce, in particular in the context of potential employment of AI specialists from abroad,
- improvement of the educational potential in digital technology by skillful talent management in the AI area,
- creation of an internationally competitive environment attracting investment such as venture capital in digital startup organizations,
- investment such as venture capital in digital startup organizations,
- construction of a modern, i.e. de-bureaucratized public administration, using new models of digital state institution management,
- promotion of initiatives for the internationalization of Brazilian startups.

g) **digital transformation of government administration**. The basic objective of this task is to make the government administration more dynamic, efficient, flexible and closer to Brazilian society. To achieve that, it is necessary to aim at the highest possible digitization of public administration, by: the development of data communication infrastructure in state offices, implementation of advanced applications and systems employing AI-based solutions, launching remote work and electronic circulation of documents, launching platforms for the acquisition of information by applicants and resolving competitions and tenders. The aspirations of the Brazilian authorities in the context of digitization of state office operations will require the following actions:

- widespread online provision of all benefits and services performed by the government administration,
- preparation of tools that will help in analyzing, assessing and monitoring digital state administration management,
- promotion of digitization of processes in all public administration bodies in Brazil,

- preparation of policies protecting the functioning of public administration bodies against cyber-attacks, personal data extortions, financial fraud, etc.,
- promotion of business ecosystems,
- unification of government platforms and Digital Citizen Participation Platforms as places for e.g. improved communication and exchange of common experience.

The digital economy development strategy prepared by the Brazilian authorities is a structure that has been based on two pillars. The first one represents the enablers axis, while the other one the digital transformation axis. In reality, both create a rich set of strategic activities which, if materialized, are necessary to create and then develop Brazil's digital economy. The timeframe adopted in the strategy assumes that within five years, i.e. from 2018 to 2021, most of the planned actions can be accomplished, but this should be regarded as too optimistic. First, because the number of tasks does not really correspond to Brazil's technical and time-related potential. Second, even a short-term slowdown in the global GDP growth rate may considerably delay the implementation of the planned activities as a result of the small "regenerative" potential of the Brazilian economy. Third, the global labor market is currently suffering from a significant deficit of experts in AI or other digital technologies, and this will result in the prolonged implementation time of the projects scheduled in Brazil. And fourth, last, Brazil's potential on the international arena is perceived by investors as being significantly below the global rankings, reducing the attractiveness of this country and decreasing its competitiveness from other states. Bearing this in mind, it should expected that the time planned for the implementation of the tasks stipulated in the strategy will be prolonged by at least three to four years until approximately 2025. Only then, provided that nothing extraordinary happens, will Brazil be able to take pride in the accomplishment of a substantial portion of the actions that have been envisaged in its strategy.

4.5 Africa

Africa is presently the only continent where none of the individual states have a ready AI or digital economy development strategy (see Table 4.1). This even applies to such states as Nigeria, the Republic of South Africa, Egypt or Algeria, where societies are commonly considered as the richest and the most developed in Africa. However, this does not mean that countries in Africa are not interested in new technologies, or that AI-based solutions are exotic for them. Quite to the contrary. As an example, we can mention that in Kenya or South Africa AI tools have already been used for a long time, either in the health service, public transport, finances or agriculture. In the case of agriculture, which serves an important function for Africa from the point of view of the employment rate, for comparison, it is also worth looking at Nigeria and the company Zenvus,[33] the operations of which focus on the delivery of information to farmers, which is used to improve yields and general efficiency in agriculture. The information received by farmers from

Zenvus originates from smart sensors and is concerned, among other things, with precipitation, precise weather forecasts or the ways of improving and preventing degradation of soil. In other words, this company's operations is proof not only of the physical presence of AI tools in Africa, but also of Africans' struggle with extreme poverty using modern technologies, in this case related to AI.

Although national AI or digital economy development plans have not been worked out so far on the level of particular countries, Africa, as a continent, has a draft digital transformation strategy for Africa for 2020–30 (African Union, 2019). This document was prepared in 2019 by the African Union (AU),[34] describing a number of projects and actions intended to create a uniform digital market in Africa by 2030 under a common initiative "Intelligent Africa". In addition, it is part of a larger plan associated with transformation of Africa into a global power of the future by 2063.[35] In this context, it is beyond doubt that both AU representatives and governments of its member states are aware of the potential and the opportunities offered by digital technology in pursuing the e-economy and social welfare. It is not a secret that technological innovations related either to automation, or digitization, create workplaces, eliminate poverty, reduce the level of social inequalities as well as making it easier to deliver goods, even to the most remote places in the world. These circumstances put Africa in a good light, as the continent has in a way a "natural" capacity of absorbing everything that is new and previously unknown. In fact, the technology that will flow to Africa will be world-class technology, often better than the one possessed today by the richest nations. On the other hand, this may mean that the civilizational leap Africa wants to make in the next several decades will happen earlier than planned. However, a *sine qua non* condition for such a scenario to materialize is the joint involvement in this project of both AU representatives (at the managerial and organizational level), all governments of African states (on the operational and executive level) and African social and economic and financial organizations, including World Bank representatives (at the level of advisors and experts). Only such an approach, based on shared and coordinated activities, will allow African countries to reap notable benefits from the development of the Fourth Industrial Revolution[36] and thereby create "Intelligent Africa" as suggested in the AU strategy.

In the light of the conditions mentioned above, AU representatives have determined the synthetic goal to be pursued by African countries in building a modern economy by 2030. In practice, its accomplishment is to rely on taking advantage of the potential offered by modern digital technologies in transforming African national economies and their societies. These changes are to give rise to the generated higher economic growth that will foster inclusion of societies into economic circulation, creation of new workplaces, removal of the digital gap and elimination of poverty in order to ensure that African states can derive the benefits from the Fourth Industrial Revolution for the social and economic development of the whole of mankind (African Union, 2019). On the other hand, the pursuit of the general goal is to be supported by actions and tasks that have been defined in the detailed (operating) objectives, related to e.g. (African Union, 2019):

- **first** – building a uniform digital market in Africa by 2030,
- **second** – building a data communication infrastructure with access to safe and fast Internet on the African continent by 2030. As part of this task, the following parameters were specified: Internet speed of min. 6 MB/s, price for using the Internet not higher than USD 0.01/1 MB, devices (produced in Africa) for using the Internet not more expensive than USD 100/per unit,
- **third** – promotion of the sharing economy, which is to contribute to stronger trade and inflow of capital and investment to Africa,
- **fourth** – creating an environment that will be conducive to securing funds for goals related to bridging the gap in IT infrastructure and access to an affordable, safe broadband Internet connection regardless of age, sex and place of residence,
- **fifth** – preparation and standardization of policies, laws and regulations which will be the foundation for animating and developing Africa's digital transformation on the continental, national, regional as well as local levels,
- **sixth** – adoption by the AU member states of the principles concerning the legal regulations in the areas of e-transactions, personal data protection, privacy, consumer protection, cybercrime and protection of copyright and intellectual property,
- **seventh** – implementation of the digital management framework at the level of AU states,
- **eighth** – promotion and protection of national top-level domains (Country Codes Top Level Domains, ccTLD)[37] as an economic asset of critical nature,
- **ninth** – building integrated digital abilities among societies regarding: programming, data analysis, machine learning, artificial intelligence, robotics, engineering, innovation, entrepreneurship, quantum mechanics, computing systems etc.,
- **tenth** – delivering basic skills in using the Internet for almost 1 billion Africans by 2025,
- **eleventh** – building an environment conducive to the development of the digital labor market,
- **twelfth** – creating a platform for the digital integration of various fields, in which representatives of public administration, the private sector as well as social organizations and civil movements will be involved, in order to maximize the social and economic benefits resulting from the digitization of states and entire societies,
- **thirteenth** – support, under Agenda 2063,[38] of the development programs of policies and strategies leading to the formation of e-services, e-applications, e-medicine, e-administration, e-payments, e-science etc.,
- **fourteenth** – putting pressure above all on the digitization of agriculture, health, education and public administration (99.9 percent of the African population should have a digital legal identity by 2030),
- **fifteenth** – planning and implementing financing models for the digital transformation in Africa, broken into two stages: stage one, 2020–25, with investment of USD 20 billion and stage two, 2026–30, with investment of USD 30

billion. In total in the years 2020–30 in Africa the level of investment in the development of the digital economy and AI is to reach nearly USD 50 billion.

The number of tasks that have been prepared under the "Intelligent Africa" strategy by AU representatives is not only significant and requires large financial outlays, but is also a civilizational challenge for all states forming this continent. The scale and the size of this project are unparalleled in Africa's most recent history. This means that if the states on this continent want to make use of the potential offered by digital technology and the related development of the Fourth Industrial Revolution, they must be determined to take up the tasks, which primarily will be:

- increase the consistency and harmonization of actions in the implementation of Africa's digital strategy at the continental, national, regional and local levels,
- increase the number and the pace of implementation of economic reforms being key for this project, in the area of education, law and international cooperation,
- increase the financial outlays for education and digital projects,
- result in a permanent growth in expenses on research and development in relation to GDP, as in most African states this indicator oscillates below 0.25 percent of GDP.[39]

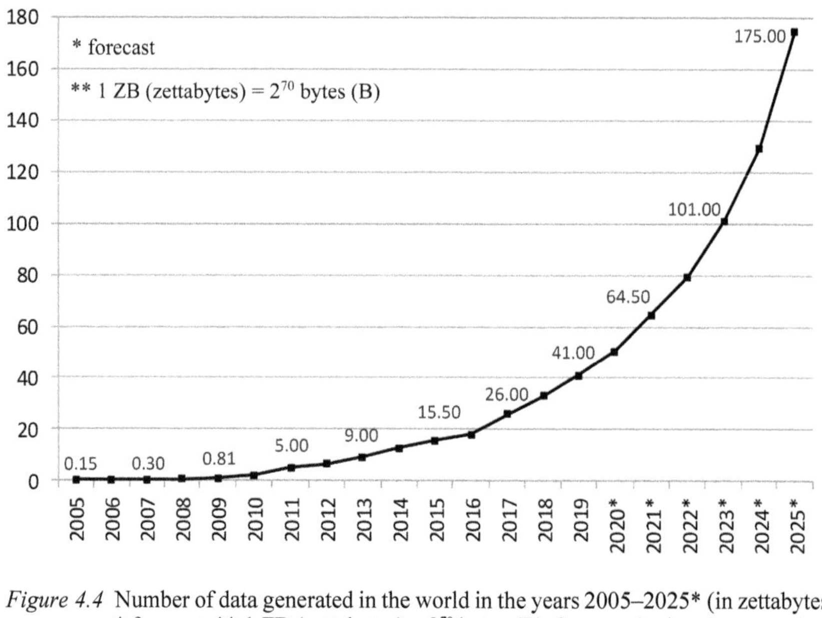

Figure 4.4 Number of data generated in the world in the years 2005–2025* (in zettabytes). * forecast. ** 1 ZB (zettabytes) = 2^{70} bytes (B). Source: Authors' own study on the basis of: statista 2020.

It should also be expected that the implementation of these tasks in Africa will be fostered by the worldwide growing accessibility of cellular telephony and the Internet, especially as the price for access to these technologies, in fact from the moment of their emergence, has been continuously going down. However, it seems that a crucial issue for the development of digital technology in Africa, in particular AI, will also be African states' access to global data resources, the size of which is already counted in dozens of zettabytes worldwide (see Figure 4.4).

Notes

1 Downloaded from: https://www.whitehouse.gov/ai/.(01.03.2020).
2 Applies to transfer of data from system A to system B regardless of the distance between them.
3 It is concerned with the application of codes and IDs to ensure that the information is clearly understandable for system A and system B.
4 Applies to coordination of processes under the systems held by the organization, which enables their mutual cooperation.
5 For more information, see: https://www.darpa.mil/.
6 Read more in Smith-Goodson (2019).
7 For more information, see: Ministry of Civil Affairs of the People's Republic of China (http://www.mca.gov.cn/).
8 From this year on, the economy of China is dynamically developing, and its annual GDP growth is always above 6 percent year-on-year. According to the Chinese statistical office, in 2019 the GDP growth slowed down to 6.1 percent of GDP, being a result not recorded in this country for nearly three decades.
9 Namely from 1990.
10 Published by World Population Review.
11 At the same time "0" means ideal social equality, on the other hand, "1" represents ideal inequality. Therefore, the lower the Gini coefficient, the smaller the economic stratification in the society, and vice versa.
12 By 2030 China wants to become the global leader in the AI domain and the market related to this technology in this country is to grow to USD 150 billion.
13 CNY 1000.00 = USD 143.37 (the average exchange rate of the National Bank of Poland of 12 March 2020).
14 As above.
15 The official name of this document is: "The White Paper on Artificial Intelligence. The European Approach to Excellence and Trust".
16 Before the White Paper was created in 2020, the EU published five other, AI technology-related, important documents, including: Declaration of cooperation on AI – in April 2018 (*Declaration of cooperation on Artificial Intelligence*), Artificial intelligence for Europe – in April 2018 (*Artificial Intelligence for Europe*), Ethics guidelines for trustworthy AI – April 2019 (*Ethics guidelines for trustworthy AI*), Policy and investment recommendations for trustworthy Artificial Intelligence – April 2019 (*Policy and investment recommendations for trustworthy Artificial Intelligence*) and the European Alliance Assembly – June 2019 (*The European Alliance Assembly*). For more information, see: (Moltzau, 2019).
17 The tourist industry in Europe directly accounts for generating more than 5% of the GDP in the EU, and the number of enterprises forming this sector reaches nearly 1.9 million.
18 According to The Forbes Global 2000 list, in 2019 as many as 575 of the largest companies worldwide came from the United States. For comparison, from Japan and South Korea, respectively: 223 and 62.
19 The budget of this program reaches EUR 8.1 billion.

20 The budget of this program reaches EUR 100 billion.
21 The basic task of the fund established in 1994 is to support and create the SME sector within the EU structures.
22 The budget of this program reaches EUR 100 million.
23 It is to foster, first of all, a broad exchange of data between sectors in the EU; second, respect for the European personal data protection law, the principles of competition or the right to privacy; and third, general access of all EU citizens to data, provided on clearly defined principles.
24 Members of the G-20 group are Argentina, Australia, Brazil, Canada, China, France, Germany, Italy, India, Indonesia, Japan, Mexico, Republic of Korea, Russia, Saudi Arabia, the Republic of South Africa, Turkey, the UK, the United States and the European Union. In total the group accounts for 90 percent of the GDP worldwide.
25 World Trade Organization.
26 International Telecommunication Union. It is the oldest international organization in the world, established in 1865.
27 For more information, see: https://www.un.org/sustainabledevelopment/sustainable-development-goals/.
28 For more information, see: http://memoria.rnp.br/pd/giga/.
29 See Note 22 in Chapter 1.
30 Program of Human Resources in Strategic Areas – a human resource development program in strategic areas of the economy.
31 MERCOSUR (*Mercado Común del Sur*) is the largest free trade zone in South America associating as full members: Argentina, Brazil, Paraguay and Uruguay.
32 BRICS is a group of states represented by Brazil, Russia, India, China and the Republic of South Africa that joined this group in 2011.
33 For more information, see: https://www.zenvus.com.
34 The African Union is an international organization composed of 55 member states being countries on the African continent. AU started its operations in 2002, at the same time being the successor of the Organization of African Unity operating on the African continent in the period 1963–99.
35 This plan has been formulated under the Agenda 2063 project. On the other hand, the date adopted in it reflects the execution of these activities within the upcoming 50 years, counting from May 2013, marking the golden anniversary of the establishment of the Organization of African Unity and then the African Union.
36 For more information, see Chapter 1.3.
37 It is a two-letter domain reserved for a particular state or dependent territory (e.g. .pl – for Poland, .us – for the United States of America, .cn – for the People's Republic of China). In practice, the .cd domain is used only by the Democratic Republic of the Congo, and, consequently, it should not be used to any extent e.g. by companies involved in the production of compact discs – CDs. At the same time, the abbreviation .cd cannot be present in the domain of any of the aforementioned companies, unless it is a company operating on the territory of the Democratic Republic of the Congo.
38 For more information, see Chapter 1.3.
39 For comparison, in highly developed countries it reaches more than 2.5 percent of the GDP, and leaders spend even more than 3.5 percent of the GDP on research and development annually.

References

African Union. (2019). *The Draft Digital Transformation Strategy for Africa: DTS (2020–2030)*. Addis Ababa, Ethiopia. Downloaded 1 May 2020 from: https://au.int/.

Cai, Y. (2013). Chinese higher Education: The changes in the past two decade and reform tendencies up to 2020. In L. d. c. Ferreira & J. a. G. Albuquerque (Eds.), *China and Brasil: Challenges and Opportunities*. Campinas: Anablumme.

European Commission. (2020). *White Paper on Artificial Intelligence: A European Approach to Excellence and Trust*. Brussels: European Commission.

Gill, I. (2020). Whoever leads in artificial intelligence in 2030 will rule the world until 2100. *Future Development*. World Bank and Brookings Institution blog. Downloaded 10 March 2020 from: https://www.brookings.edu/blog/future-development/2020/01/17/whoever-leads-in-artificial-intelligence-in-2030-will-rule-the-world-until-2100/.

He, J. (2017). The next generation AI development plan: What's inside? Downloaded 10 March 2020 from: https://medium.com/@jiahe/the-next-generation-ai-development-plan-whats-inside-72824a9bcc3.

Ministry of Science, Technology, Innovation and Communications (MCTIC). (2018). *Brazilian Digital Transformation Strategy (E-Digital)*. Brasília. Distrito Federal: MCTIC.

Moltzau, A. (2019). *AI Strategy in EU Towards 2020. A Summary of the Various Strategies and Policies Relating to Artificial Intelligence 2018–2019*. Towards data science. Downloaded 20 March 2020 from: https://towardsdatascience.com/ai-strategy-in-eu-2018-201944393b7eaf28?gi=62a936eacf9e.

National Quantum Coordination Office (NQCO). (2020). *A Strategic Vision for America's Quantum Networks*. Washington, DC: The White House National Quantum Coordination Office.

Office of Science and Technology Policy (OSTP). (2020). *President Trump's FY 2021 Budget Commits to Double Investments in Key Industries of the Future*. The White House Office of Science and Technology Policy - OSTP. Downloaded 3 March 2020 from: https://www.whitehouse.gov/briefings-statements/president-trumps-fy-2021-budget-commits-double-investments-key-industries-future/.

Select Committee on Artificial Intelligence of the National Science & Technology Council. (2019). *The National Artificial Intelligence Research and Development Strategic Plan: 2019 Update*. Washington, DC: The White House.

The State Council of China. (2017). *Notice of the State Council Issuing the New Generation of Artificial Intelligence Development Plan*. State Council Document No. 35. The State Council of China.

Summary

There are probably very few people in the world who would be willing to question the statement that we are living in the artificial intelligence era. Its influence is so strong and ubiquitous that some researchers even forecast a **total world of artificial intelligence**. Their use of the word "total" makes us, more and more often, ask questions about ethics, moral principles and our safety in the context of the application of such technologies. This happens because it is the **totality** of things, being pejorative in meaning, that brings forth our concerns, reluctance and sometimes even fear. However, on a daily basis most of us do not attach any greater importance to this type of discussion nor to perceptions of artificial intelligence as a technology that may threaten human existence. Furthermore, there are even those who almost ostentatiously confess, to paraphrase the French molecular biologist and writer J. de Rosnay, that more than artificial intelligence, in life they are afraid of natural (read: human) stupidity. Setting such an approach aside, it is undisputed that artificial intelligence is a technology that, utilizing digital resources in the form of uncountable data volumes, is used to predict the future, identify items and persons as well as monitor processes and behaviors of both machines and people. In the case of devices and their ability to learn and perform tasks independently, this technology is perceived, mostly by scientists, technologists as well as business leaders, as one of the most transformational worldwide.

The aim of this book was to provide a holistic perspective on management problems, including management of organizational development, in light of the development of its new environment, associated with the blossoming of artificial intelligence technology. In research for this book, which utilized, among others: scientific magazines, monographs, conference materials, industry reports, focus interviews and group interviews with representatives of world corporations, scientific and industry journals as well as webinars, an attempt was made to respond to problems related to the functioning and management of the organization in the era of deep transformations caused by the development of artificial intelligence technologies. In particular, these included an attempt to explain issues related to:

- the impact of artificial intelligence on organizations, business and management in the postmodern era,

DOI: 10.4324/9781003184027-102

- the effect of the organization on turbulent changes in its organizational environment, both immediate and distant,
- intra-structural changes in the organizational framework,
- construction of a new type of artificial intelligence-based organization in the world of management, utilizing AI solutions in everyday activity,
- construction and management of innovative business ecosystems, including the net ecosystem,
- modeling of artificial intelligence development stages,
- modeling of data processing methods in artificial intelligence-based organizations,
- formation of a new management paradigm associated with the impact of artificial intelligence technologies on organizations,
- construction of national strategies for artificial intelligence implementation.

In the opinion of the authors, this attempt to answer these and many other questions as formulated in this publication should be considered successful and it will hopefully encounter a kind reception from the readers. Simultaneously, we must be aware that the topic being discussed, due to its complexity and multi-faceted nature, does not fully exhaust the issue of managing organizations and artificial intelligence technology. This is even more the case because this problem area is still vibrant, and artificial intelligence, as a technology and a field of knowledge, is subject to continuous transformations and development. This situation creates further, new opportunities to enrich present knowledge in this area, which, in the opinion of the authors, should be focused on the problems and research related to the development, this time not of the artificial intelligence era, but of the quantum technology era.

Bibliography

Accenture. (2018). A technology revolution like no other. In *Explained a Guide for Executives*. New Jersey: Accenture Applied Intelligence.

African Union. (2019). *The Draft Digital Transformation Strategy for Africa: DTS (2020–2030)*. Addis Ababa, Ethiopia. Downloaded 1 May 2020 from: https://au.int/.

AiLab. (2019). *AiLab Artificial Intelligence Glossary*. Downloaded 12 September 2019 from: https://www.ailab.com.au/resources/ai-glossary/.

Anderl, R. (2014). Industrie 4.0: Advanced engineering of smart products and smart production. In 19° Seminário Internacional de Alta Tecnologia – Inovações Tecnológicas no Desenvolvimento do Produto, Piracicaba, Brasil.

Aon. (2019). *The Future of Business: How Artificial Intelligence Can Drive Organizational Change*. TheOneBrief. Downloaded 20 November 2019 from: https://theonebrief.com/the-future-of-business-how-artificial-intelligence-can-drive-organizational-change/.

Bellman, R. (1978). *An Introduction to Artificial Intelligence: Can Computers Think?* San Francisco: Boyd & Fraser Publishing Company.

Blanche, M., Rinn, T., Von Thaden, G., & De Thieulloy, G. (2014). *Industry 4.0. The New Industrial Revolution: How Europe Will Succeed*. Munich: Roland Berger Strategy Consultants GMBH.

Boucher, P. (2019). *How Artificial Intelligence Works*. European Parliamentary Research Service. Scientific Foresight Unit (STOA). Panel for the Future of Science and Technology.

Bowser, A., Sloan, M., Michelucci, P., & Pauwels, E. (2017). *Artificial Intelligence: A Policy-Oriented Introduction*. Washington, DC: The Wilson Center.

Buła, P., & Nogalski, B. (Eds.). (2020). *The Future of Management: Industry 4.0 and Digitalization*. Kraków: Jagiellonian University Press.

Buła, P., & Schroeder, T. (2020). Wpływ wybranych aspektów czwartej rewolucji przemysłowej na zmiany w ekosystemie biznesu. In M. Urbaniak, & A. Tomaszewski (Eds.), *Wyzwania społeczne i technologiczne a nowe trendy w zarządzaniu współczesnymi organizacjami*. Warszawa: Szkoła Główna Handlowa w Warszawie, pp. 33–45.

Buła, P., Dziedzic, D., & Uznańska, M. (2020). Mathematical risk assessment method in the implementation of logistic processes. In P. Buła, & B. Nogalski (Eds.), *The Future of Management: Industry 4.0 and Digitalization*. Kraków: Jagiellonian University Press, pp. 161–177.

BusinessNews Publishing. (2014). *Summary: The Mesh: Review and Analysis of Gansky's Book*. Cambridge, MA: Primento.

Cai, Y. (2013). Chinese higher Education: The changes in the past two decade and reform tendencies up to 2020. In L. d. c. Ferreira & J. a. G. Albuquerque (Eds.), *China and Brasil: Challenges and Opportunities*. Campinas: Anablumme.

Deloitte A. G. (2015). *Industry 4.0. Challenges and Solutions for the Digital Transformation and Use of Exponential Technologies*. Zurich: The Creative Studio at Deloitte.

Dombrowski, U., & Wagner T. (2014). Mental strain as field of action in the 4th industrial revolution. *Procedia CIRP*, *17*, pp. 100–105.

Ernst, E., Merola, R., & Samaan, D. (2018). *The Economics of Artificial Intelligence: Implications for the Future of Work*. ILO Future of Work Research Paper Series. Geneva, Switzerland: The International Labour Office.

Etzioni, O. (2016). *No, the Experts Don't Think Superintelligent AI is a Threat to Humanity*. MIT Technology Review. Downloaded 12 September 2019 from: https://www.tec hnologyreview.com/s/602410/no-the-experts-dont-think-superintelligent-aiis-a-threat -tohumanity/.

European Commission. (2016). *Research Workshop on Digitising the Agri-food Sector: A Research Agenda for Horizon 2020*. Brussels: Directorate General for Agriculture and Rural Development. Downloaded from: https://ec.europa.eu/newsroom/horizon2020/ document.cfm?doc_id=40233.

European Commission. (2020). *White Paper on Artificial Intelligence: A European Approach to Excellence and Trust*. Brussels: European Commission.

Flex International Ltd. (2019). *How Industry 4.0 Will Virtually Erase Downtime and Save You Money*. Downloaded 1 August 2019 from: https://flex.com/insights/live-smarter-b log/how industry-40-will-virtually-erase-downtime-and-save-you-money.

Fonseca, L. M. (2018). Industry 4.0 and the digital society: Concepts, dimensions and envisioned benefits. In Proceedings of the International Conference on Business Excellence, Porto, Portugal, Vol. 12, pp. 386–395. DOI: 10.2478/picbe-2018-0034.

Friedmann, G. (1936). *La Crise du progrès: esquisse d'histoire des idées, 1895–1935*. Paris: Gallimard.

Gansky, L. (2010). *The Mesh: Why the Future of Business Is Sharing*. New York: Portfolio Penguin.

Gill, I. (2020). Whoever leads in artificial intelligence in 2030 will rule the world until 2100. *Future Development*. World Bank and Brookings Institution blog. Downloaded 10 March 2020 from: https://www.brookings.edu/blog/future-development/2020/01/17 /whoever-leads-in-artificial-intelligence-in-2030-will-rule-the-world-until-2100/.

Gillham, J., Rimmington, L., Dance, H., Verweij, G., Rao, A., Roberts, K. B., & Paich, M. (2018). *The Macroeconomic Impact of Artificial Intelligence*. London: PwC.

Glass, R., Meissner, A., Gebauer, Ch., Sturmer, S., & Metternich, J. (2018). Identifying the barriers to Industrie 4.0. In 51st CIRP Conference on Manufacturing Systems, Stockholm, Sweden.

Hartikainen, J., & Virtanen, M. (2019). Management paradigms in a nutshell. Downloaded 30 November 2019 from: https://www.tieto.com/en/blog/2019/07/management-paradi gms-in-a-nutshell/.

He, J. (2017). The next generation AI development plan: What's inside? Downloaded 10 March 2020 from: https://medium.com/@jiahe/the-next-generation-ai-development -plan-whats-inside-72824a9bcc3.

Hermann, M., Pentek, T., & Otto, B. (2016). Design principles for Industrie 4.0 scenarios. In 49th Hawaii International Conference on System Sciences, IEEE, Koloa, HI, USA.

Kagermann, H., Wahlster, W., & Helbig, J. (2013). *Recommendations for Implementing the Strategic Initiative Industrie 4.0*. Linda Treugut, M.A. and acatech - Frankfurt/ Main: National Academy of Science and Engineering.

Kelner, D., & Kostadinov, A. (2019). *The State of AI 2019: Divergence*. London: MMC Ventures Research.

Kolbjørnsrud, V., Amico, R., & Thomas, R. J. (2016a). How artificial intelligence will redefine management. *Harvard Business Review*. Downloaded 1 December 2019 from: https://hbr.org/2016/11/how-artificial-intelligence-will-redefine-management.

Kolbjørnsrud, V., Amico, R., & Thomas, R. J. (2016b). *The Promise of Artificial Intelligence. Redefining Management in the Workforce of the Future*. Oslo: Accenture.

Kuznets, S. (1965). *Economic Growth and Structure*. New York: W.W. Nortonan.

Latentview. (2018). How to make artificial intelligence work for your organization. *Business Analytics*. Downloaded 4 September 2019 from: https://www.latentview.com /blog/business-benefit-from-ai/.

Lele, A. (2019). Debating lethal autonomous weapon systems. Institute for defence studies and analyses. *J. Def. Stud.*, *13*(1), January–March, pp. 51–70.

Lewin, N. (2017). *All Change for Industry 4.0*. Denkendorf: Festo Training & Consulting.

Li, W., Wu, W. J., Wang, H. M., Cheng, X. J., Chen, H. J., Zhou, Z. H., & Ding, R. (2017). Crowd intelligence in AI 2.0 era. *Front. Inform. Technol. Electron. Eng.*, 18(1), pp. 15–43. DOI: org/10.1631/FITEE.1601859.

Liffler, M., & Tschiesner, A. (2013). *The Internet of Things and the Future of Manufacturing*. Stuttgart, Munich: McKinsey & Company.

Lorenz, P., & Saslow, K. (2019). *Demystifying AI & AI Companies. What Foreign Policy Makers Need to Know about the Global AI Industry*. Berlin: Stiftung Neue Verantwortung e.V.

Manyika, J., & Bughin, J. (2018). *The Promise and Challenge of the Age of Artificial Intelligence*. San Francisco: McKinsey Global Institute.

Maslarić, M., Nikoličić, S., & Mirčetić, D. (2016). Logistics response to the industry 4.0: The physical internet. *Open Eng.*, *6*, pp. 511–517. DOI: 10.1515/eng-2016-0073.

McKinsey & Company. (2016). *Industry 4.0 after the Initial Hype. Where Manufacturers are Finding Value and How They Can Best Capture It*. Berlin: McKinsey Digital.

Middleton, J., McCahon, W., Rosenshine, K., Jonem, J., Cawthorne, H., & Duncan, A. (2019). *Artificial Intelligence in Financial Services*. London: UK Finance.

Ministry of Science, Technology, Innovation and Communications (MCTIC). (2018). *Brazilian Digital Transformation Strategy (E-Digital)*. Brasília. Distrito Federal: MCTIC.

Mokyr, J., & Strotz, H. R. (2000). *The Second Industrial Revolution, 1870–1914*. Downloaded 1 June 2019 from: https://www.semanticscholar.org/paper.

Moltzau, A. (2019). *AI Strategy in EU Towards 2020. A Summary of the Various Strategies and Policies Relating to Artificial Intelligence 2018–2019*. Towards data science. Downloaded 20 March 2020 from: https://towardsdatascience.com/ai-strategy-in-eu-2 018-201944393b7eaf28?gi=62a936eacf9e.

Morrison, E (2016). *Moving our Innovation Thinking from Barriers to Ecosystems*. Florence, AL: Agile Strategy Lab Network, University and the University of North Alabama.

National Quantum Coordination Office (NQCO). (2020). *A Strategic Vision for America's Quantum Networks*. Washington, DC: The White House National Quantum Coordination Office.

Nazri, A., Azim Abd Ghani, A., Hafez, I., & Ng, K. Y. (2018). A new theoretical framework for testing consciousness in a machine. In International Conference on Soft Computing and Data Mining (SCDM, 2018). Recent Advances on Soft Computing and Data Mining, pp. 330–339. Malaysia. Johor.

Organisation for Economic Co-operation and Development. (2016). *OECD Science, Technology and Innovation Outlook 2016*. Paris: OECD Publishing. Downloaded from: https://www.ewivlaanderen.be/sites/default/files/bestanden/oecd_science_technology_and_innovation_outlook_2016.pdf.

Oesterreich, T. D., & Teuteberg, F. (2016). Understanding the implications of digitisation and automation in the context of Industry 4.0: A triangulation approach and elements of a research agenda for the construction industry. *Computers in Industry*, *83*, pp. 121–139.

Office of Science and Technology Policy (OSTP). (2020). *President Trump's FY 2021 Budget Commits to Double Investments in Key Industries of the Future*. The White House Office of Science and Technology Policy - OSTP. Downloaded 3 March 2020 from: https://www.whitehouse.gov/briefings-statements/president-trumps-fy-2021-budget-commits-double-investments-key-industries-future/.

Opher, A., Chou, A., Onda, A., & Sounderrajan, K. (2016). *The Rise of the Data Economy: Driving Value through Internet of Things Data Monetization*. A Perspective for Chief Digital Officers and Chief Technology Officers. New York: IBM Global Services.

Pan, Y. (2016). Heading toward artificial intelligence 2.0. *Engineering*, *2*, pp. 409–413.

Pan, Y. (2017). Special issue on Artificial intelligence 2.0. *Front. Inf. Technol. Electron. Eng.*, *18*(1), pp. 1–2. DOI: 10.1631/FITEE.1710000.

Paschek, D., Luminosu, C. T., & Draghici, A. (2017). Automated business process management: In times of digital transformation using machine learning or artificial intelligence. In MATEC Web of Conferences, Sibiu, Romania. DOI: 10.1051/matecconf/20171210.

Patrizio, A. (2019). These artificial intelligence companies are advancing this emerging tech through myriad developments of AI systems. Downloaded 4 November 2019 from: https://www.datamation.com/artificial-intelligence/top-artificial-intelligence-companies.html.

Pei, J., Deng, L., Song, S., Zhao, M., Zhang, Y., Wu, S., Wang, G., Zou, Z., Wu, Z., Wei, H., Chen, F., Deng, N., Wu, S., Wang, Y., Wu, Y., Yang, Z., Ma, Ch., Li, G., Han, W., Li, H., Wu, H., Zhao, R., Xie, Y., & Shi, L. (2019). Towards artificial general intelligence with hybrid Tianjic chip architecture. *Nature*, *572*, pp. 106–111.

Perez, J. A., Deligianni, F., Ravi, D., & Yang G. Z. (2017). *Artificial Intelligence and Robotics*. UK-RAS White Papers. London: UK-RAS Network Robotics and Autonomous Systems.

Petrillo, A., De Felice, F., Cioffi, R., & Zomparelli, F. (2018). Fourth industrial revolution: Current practices, challenges, and opportunities. In Antonella Petrillo, Raffaele Cioffi & Fabio De Felice (Eds.), *Digital Transformation in Smart Manufacturing*, *IntechOpen*, p. 10. DOI: 10.5772/intechopen.72304.

Pink, D. H. (2009). *Drive: The Surishing Truth About What Motivates Us*. New York: Riverhead Books.

Polish Ministry of Digitization (2018). *Assumptions for the AI strategy in Poland*. Warsaw, Poland: Polish Ministry of Digitization.

Pottin, F., & Dietz, T. (2018). Automation goes 4.0: The"SMART"AACfactory. *Ce/papers, 2018*, pp. 25–28. DOI: org/10.1002/cepa.898.

Purdy, M., & Daugherty, P. (2016). *Why Artificial Intelligence is the Future of Growth*. Accenture.

PwC. (2016). *Industry 4.0: Building the Digital Enterprise*. Munich, Gemany: PwC.

Rajkumar, R., Lee, I., Sha, L., & Stankovic, J. (2010) Cyber-physical systems: The next computing revolution. In Design Automation Conference 2010, Anaheim, CA.

Ransbotham, S., Khodabandeh, S., Fehling, R., LaFountain, B., & Kiron, D. (2019). *Winning With AI. Pioneers Combine Strategy, Organizational Behavior, and Technology*. Cambridge: MIT Sloan Management Review and Boston Consulting Group.

Revell, T. (2017). AI will be able to beat us at everything by 2060, say expert. *New Scientist*. Downloaded 12 September 2019 from: https://www.newscientist.com/article/2133188-ai-will-be-able-to-beat-us-at-everything-by-2060-say-experts/.

Rifkin, J. (2012). The third industrial revolution: How the internet, green electricity, and 3-D printing are ushering in a sustainable era of distributed capitalism. *World Financ. Rev., 2012*, pp. 8–12.

Saxena, A., & Gopal, K. S. (2013). Quantum artificial consciousness. In Conference: Emerging Trends in Computer Science Research and Developement (ETCRD), Haridwar, Volume: Special Volume.

Schatsky, D., Camhi, J., & Muraskin, C. (2019). *Data Ecosystems: How Third-Party Information Can Enhance Data Analytics*. New York: Deloitte Development LLC.

Schröder, Ch. (2017). *The Challenges of Industry 4.0 for Small and Medium-sized Enterprises*. Bonn: Friedrich-Ebert-Stiftung, Division for Economic and Social Policy.

Schroeder, T., & Ziółko, M. (2020). Renewable energy through industry 4.0 on the example of photovoltaic development in selected European countries. In P. Buła, & B. Nogalski (Eds.), *The Future of Management: Industry 4.0 and Digitalization*. Kraków: Jagiellonian University Press, pp. 92–107.

Schwab, K. (2016). *The Fourth Industrial Revolution*. Cologny/Geneva: Penguin Books Ltd.

Select Committee on Artificial Intelligence of the National Science & Technology Council. (2019). *The National Artificial Intelligence Research and Development Strategic Plan: 2019 Update*. Washington, DC: The White House.

Seseña Gaitán, D., & López Martínez, Í. (2017). Five errors in the implementation of Industry 4.0. How to be ready for the digitalization roll-out. Downloaded 1 September 2019 from: https://www.minsait.com/sites/default/files/newsroom_documents/five_errors_in_the_implementation_of_industry_4.pdf.

Shabbir, J., & Anwer, T. (2015). Artificial intelligence and its role in near future. *J. Latex Class Files, 14*(8), pp. 1–11.

Siemens. (2017). Od industry 4.0 do smart factory. Downloaded 1 August 2019 from: https://www.siemens.pl/industry-40.

Siljebrìt, H., Addyman, C., & Pickering, A. (2018). Towards human-like artificial intelligence using StarCraft 2. In Foundations of Digital Games 2018 (FDG18), August 7–10, 2018, Malmö, Sweden. New York: ACM. DOI: org/10.1145/3235765.3235811.

Sirimanne, S. N., Fredriksson, T., Fajarnes-Garces, P., Fondeur-Gil, S., Jones, Ch., Julsaint-Kidane, M., Korka, D., & Van Giffen, T. (2019). Digital economy report 2019. Value creation and capture: Implications for developing countries. In United Nations Conference on Trade and Development, New York.

Smit, J., Kreutzer, S., Moeller, C., & Carlberg, M. (2016). *Industry 4.0* (Report No. IP/A/ITRE/2015-02). Brussels: European Parliament, Directorate-General for Internal Policies.

Smith-Goodson, P. (2019). *Quantum USA Vs. Quantum China: The World's Most Important Technology Race*. Moor Insights and Strategy. Jersey City, NJ: Forbes.

Szczepański, M. (2019). *Economic Impacts of Artificial Intelligence (AI)*. Brussels: European Parliamentary Research Service, EPRS. European Parliament.

The Economist (2019). *The AI-enabled Organisation of the Future*. London: The Economist Intelligence Unit Ltd.

The State Council of China. (2017). *Notice of the State Council Issuing the New Generation of Artificial Intelligence Development Plan*. State Council Document No. 35. The State Council of China.

Tian, Y. H., Chen, X. L., Xiong, H. K., Li, H. L., Dai, L. R., Chen, J., Xing, J. L., Chen, J., Wu, X. H., Hu, W. M., Hu, Y., Huang, T. J., & Gao, W. (2017). Towards human-like and transhuman perception in AI 2.0: A review. *Front. Inform. Technol. Electron. Eng.*, *18*(1), pp. 58–67.

United Nations Conference on Trade and Development. (2017). *Digitalization, Trade and Development*. Information Economy Report 2017. Geneva: UNCTAD. Downloaded 1 December 2019 from: https://unctad.org/en/PublicationsLibrary/ier2017_en./ier2017_en.pdf.

United Nations Industrial Development Organization (UNIDO). (2017). Industry 4.0: The opportunities behind the challenge. In General Conference, Partnering for Impact: Achieving the Sustainable Development Goals, Department of Trade, Investment and Innovation, Vienna International Centre, Vienna, Austria. United Nations Industrial Development Organization (UNIDO).

Winberg, E., & Ahrén, J. (2018). *Industry 4.0 from a Technology Adoption Perspective*. Stockholm: The Royal Institute of Technology.

Wong, S., Wan, J., Li, D., & Zhang, C. (2016). Implementing smart factory of industry 4.0: An outlook. *Int. J. Distrib. Sens. Netwo.*, *12*(1), p. 2. DOI: org/10.1155/2016/3159805.

Xu, M., David, J. M., & Hi Kim, S. (2018). The fourth industrial revolution: Opportunities and challenges. *Int. J. Financ. Res.*, *9*, pp. 90–94. DOI: 10.5430/ijfr.v9n2p90.

Xue, J. R., Wang, D., Du, S. Y., Cui, D. X., Huang, Y., & Zheng, N. N. (2017). A vision-centered multi-sensor fusing approach to self-localization and obstacle perception for robotic cars. *Front. Inform. Technol. Electron. Eng.*, *18*(1), pp. 122–138. DOI: org/10.1631/FITEE.1601873.

Yao, X. et al. (2017). Smart manufacturing based on cyber-physical systems and beyond. *J. Intell. Manuf.* (Peer-reviewed), 13 December, *30*, p. 13.

Zhang, T., Li, Q., Zhang, C. S., Liang, H. W., Li, P., Wang, T. M., Shuo, L., Zhu, Y. L., & Cheng, W. (2017). Current trends in the development of intelligent unmanned autonomous systems. *Front. Inform. Technol. Electron. Eng.*, *18*(1), pp. 68–85. DOI: org/10.1631/FITEE.1601650.

Zheng, P., et al. (2018). Smart manufacturing systems for Industry 4.0: Conceptual framework, scenarios, and future perspectives. *Front. Mech. Eng.* (Peer-reviewed), 27 September, *13*(2), pp. 137–150.

Zhou, L. K., Tang, S. L., Xiao, J., Wu, F., & Zhuang, Y. T. (2017). Disambiguating named entities with deep supervised learning via crowd labels. *Front. Inform. Technol. Electron. Eng.*, *18*(1), pp. 97–106. DOI: org/10.1631/FITEE.1601835.

Zhuang, Y. T., Wu, F., Chen, C., & Pan, Y. H. (2017). Challenges and opportunities: From big data to knowledge in AI 2.0. *Front. Inform. Technol. Electron. Eng.*, *18*(1), pp. 3–14. DOI: org/10.1631/FITEE.1601883.

Index

bold denotes tables; *italics* denotes figures

Milton Keynes UK
Ingram Content Group UK Ltd.
UKHW020949081223
433929UK00020B/415

9 781032 025834